SCIENCE ACTIVITIES

INSIDE MATTER

VOLUME 5

Colin Uttley

GROLIER
EDUCATIONAL

Published 2002 by Grolier Educational
Sherman Turnpike,
Danbury, Connecticut 06816

FOR BROWN PARTWORKS

Project editor:	Lisa Magloff
Deputy editor:	Jane Scarsbrook
Text editors:	Caroline Beattie, Leon Gray, Ben Morgan
Designer:	Joan Curtis
Picture researcher:	Liz Clachan
Illustrations:	Darren Awuah, Mark Walker
Index:	Kay Ollerenshaw
Design manager:	Lynne Ross
Production manager:	Matt Weyland
Managing editor:	Bridget Giles
Editorial director:	Anne O'Daly
Consultant:	Martin Wheeler, PhD University of Leicester

Printed and bound in Hong Kong

Set ISBN 0-7172-5608-1
Volume ISBN 0-7172-5613-8

Library of Congress Cataloging-in-Publication Data
Science Activities / Grolier Educational
    p. cm.
    Includes index.
    Contents: v.1. Electricity and magnetism—v.2. Everyday Chemistry—v.3. Force and motion—v.4. Heat and energy—v.5. Inside matter—v.6. Light and color—v.7. Our Environment—v.8. Sound and hearing—v.9. Using materials—v.10. Weather and climate.
ISBN 0-7172-5608-1 (set : alk.paper)—ISBN 0-7172-5609-X (v.1 : alk. paper)—
ISBN 0-7172-5610-3 (v.2 : alk. paper)—ISBN 0-7172-5611-1 (v.3 : alk. paper)—ISBN
0-7172-5612-X (v.4 : alk. paper)—ISBN 0-7172-5613-8 (v.5 : alk. paper)—ISBN
0-7172-5614- 6 (v.6 : alk. paper)—ISBN 0-7172-5615-4 (v.7 : alk. paper)—ISBN
0-7172-5616-2 (v.8 : alk. paper)—ISBN 0-7172-5617-0 (v.9 : alk. paper)—ISBN
0-7172-5618-9 (v.10 : alk. paper)
    1. Science—Study and teaching—Activity programs—Juvenile literature. [1. Science—Experiments. 2. Experiments] I. Grolier Educational (Firm)

LB1585.S335 2002
507.1'2—dc21
                                                    2001040519

ABOUT THIS SET

Science Activities gives children a chance to explore fascinating topics from the world of science using the same methods that professional scientists use to solve problems. This set introduces young scientists to the scientific method by focusing on the importance of planning experiments, conducting them in a rigorous fashion so that a fair test can be carried out, recording all the stages, and organizing and analyzing the data to draw conclusions. Readers will have the chance to conduct exciting and innovative hands-on activities and to learn how to record and analyze their experiments and results in a variety of ways.

Every volume of *Science Activities* contains 10 step-by-step experiments, along with follow-up activities that encourage readers to find out more about the subject. The activities are explained and enhanced with detailed introductory and analysis sections. Colorful photos illustrate each activity, and every book is packed full of pictures and illustrations explaining the details of each topic.

By working fun and educational experiments into the context of the scientific method, anyone using this set can get a feel for how professional scientists go about their work. Most importantly, just have fun!

CONTENTS

VOLUME 5

INSIDE MATTER

INTRODUCTION
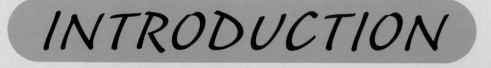

Everything is made up of matter—from stars to this book and the hands you are holding it with. Chemistry and physics both study what matter is made of, and how atoms and smaller particles combine to make different things.

M atter is anything that takes up space. Matter is arranged in forms as different as vast galaxies that take light rays hundreds of millions of years to cross, to mountains, animals, and particles a billionth of a meter across.

Matter can have physical properties such as density, melting point, boiling point, freezing point, color, or smell. It also has chemical properties. They include how easily one type of matter will combine with another type of matter to make a different type of matter.

There are four main states of matter: solid, liquid, gas, and plasma. In each state the particles of matter are different distances apart.

Matter moves from one state to another when energy is added or taken away. Energy can be added to matter in many ways, such as by increasing the temperature or pressure. Similarly, when the temperature or pressure is decreased, energy is taken away. In both cases changes occur in the structure and behavior of the matter.

Matter can be organized into structures as small as an atom and as large as this spiral galaxy (galaxy NGC 4414), imaged by the Hubble Space Telescope in 1995.

When matter moves from one state to another, its chemical properties do not change. For example, water (H_2O) is made up of two atoms of hydrogen and one atom of oxygen. If you add energy to liquid water by heating it, it will turn into a gas— water vapor. You can see water vapor form over a pot of boiling water. If the vapor loses energy to its surroundings (cools), it will condense and become a drop of liquid water. If you put that drop in the freezer, it would lose more energy and become a solid (ice). All of these are physical changes. In each case the chemical (H_2O) was unchanged. No matter what state it was in, it was always water, and it always had the same chemical properties. A chemical change, such as adding a carbon atom, would change the way the water acted, making it not water, but something completely new.

Physics is the study of the physical properties of matter, and physical changes that take place in matter, while chemistry focuses on the chemical changes that occur in matter.

It was once thought that atoms were the smallest particles of matter, and that everything else was made of atoms. Scientists then discovered that atoms were themselves made up of even smaller particles, called electrons, protons, and neutrons. The protons and neutrons are clustered together in the center, or nucleus, of the atom, and the electrons move around the nucleus like planets in orbit around a sun. The electrons "orbit" at different levels and can change their level, giving off or taking up energy as they do so. Electrons of one atom can be attracted to electrons of another atom, causing the two atoms to bond together, or share energy, and create molecules, which are combinations of atoms bonded together.

Scientists have now found that protons and neutrons are themselves made up of even tinier particles called quarks. In fact, the more physicists study particles of matter, the more particles they discover that are smaller than an atom.

In this book you will have a chance to perform experiments that will demonstrate the physical properties of matter.

■ *Solids can take many forms. This red quartz is a crystal mineral—a solid that formed deep underground, and whose atoms are arranged in a regular structure.*

The good science guide

Science is not only a collection of facts—it is the process that scientists use to gather information. Follow this good science guide to get the most out of each experiment.

● Carry out each experiment more than once. That prevents accidental mistakes skewing the results. The more times you carry out an experiment, the easier it will be to see if your results are accurate.

● Decide how you will write down your results. You can use a variety of different methods, such as descriptions, diagrams, tables, charts, and graphs. Choose the methods that will make your results easy to read and understand.

● Be sure to write your results down as you are doing the experiment. If one of the results seems very different from the others, it could be because of a problem with the experiment that you should fix immediately.

● Drawing a graph of your results can be very useful because it helps fill in the gaps in your experiment. Imagine, for example, that you plot time along the bottom of the graph and temperature up the side. If you measure the temperature ten times, you can put the results on the graph as dots. Use a ruler to draw a straight line through all the dots. You can now estimate what happened in between each dot, or measurement, by picking any point along the line and reading the time and temperature for that point from the sides of the graph.

● Learn from your mistakes. Some of the most exciting findings in science came from an unexpected result. If your results do not tally with your predictions, try to find out why.

● You should always be careful when carrying out or preparing any experiment, whether it is dangerous or not. Make sure you know the safety rules before you start working.

● Never begin an experiment until you have talked to an adult about what you are going to do.

DISSOLVING

If you drop a sugar cube into a glass of water and taste it immediately, it doesn't taste sweet. When the sugar has completely disappeared, the water tastes sweet. The sugar has spread through the water—it has dissolved.

The next time you are at the seaside, take a look at seawater. It looks clear, but it really contains many substances, such as salt and oxygen, that have dissolved into the water. Seawater is one example of a solution, a mixture in which molecules of different substances are evenly mixed together.

Solutions can be made by dissolving a solid or a gas into a liquid (or a gas). There are many examples of solutions. For example, soda pop is a solution of a solid (sugar), liquid (water, coloring, and flavoring), and a gas (carbon dioxide).

🔴 *Henna decoration. The henna plant is dried and ground, and the powder is mixed with water. The dye goes into solution, and that makes it easier to spread on and soak into the skin to dye it.*

spaced out evenly around the molecules, but in others they are shared unevenly. The first type of molecule is called nonpolar, and the second type is called polar because one end (pole) of the molecule has a slight electric charge.

Nonpolar molecules will make a solution with other nonpolar molecules, and polar molecules will make a solution with other polar molecules. In the case of oil and water the water molecules are polar, and the oil molecules are nonpolar. That is why they do not mix.

Water is a good solvent because it is polar. That means the

In any solution the substance that dissolves is called the solute. The substance the solute dissolves into is called the solvent. Whether a substance will dissolve depends on how much the molecules of the solvent and the solute are attracted to each other. That is because in some substances the electrons are molecules can form weak bonds with other charged particles. Many compounds, such as salt (sodium chloride, chemical symbol NaCl), break up in water to form two particles called ions, one with a positive charge, (Na^+), and one with a negative charge (Cl^-). Ionic substances are very soluble in water.

Nonpolar substances will not dissolve in water. Oil is one such substance—it will only dissolve in another nonpolar substance. So, solvents other than water are needed. If you have ever had tar or grease on you, you may have taken it off with gasoline, paint thinner, or cooking oil. All of them are solvents for grease and tar—they dissolve the oil.

CONCENTRATION

Solutions are described as having either a high or a low concentration. That is a way of describing how much solute there is compared with solvent. A high concentration has more solute than a low concentration. Solubility, on the other hand, is a measure of the maximum amount of a particular solute that will dissolve in a solvent at that temperature. For example, if 1 pint (500ml) of solvent will dissolve 1 ounce (14g) of solute at room temperature, its solubility is said to be 1 ounce per pint (28g/l).

When you fill a glass with water, it may look as if there is no more room in the glass, but there is really a lot of room left in between the molecules of

These terraces form when calcium carbonate dissolved in spring water comes out of solution at the surface.

water. That is why solvents dissolve solutes. The molecules in a liquid are spread out enough for the solute molecules to fit in between. If you heat the water, the molecules spread farther apart, and there is even more room for solutes, so solubility tends to increase with temperature.

Solubility

When a solute dissolves in a solvent, we say that the solute is soluble in that solvent. If a lot of the solute dissolves in a particular solvent, we say the solute has a high solubility in that solvent. If the solvent will hold only a small amount of the solute, the solute has a low solubility in that solvent. When a solid will not dissolve in a liquid, we say it is insoluble, or of two liquids, that they will not mix.

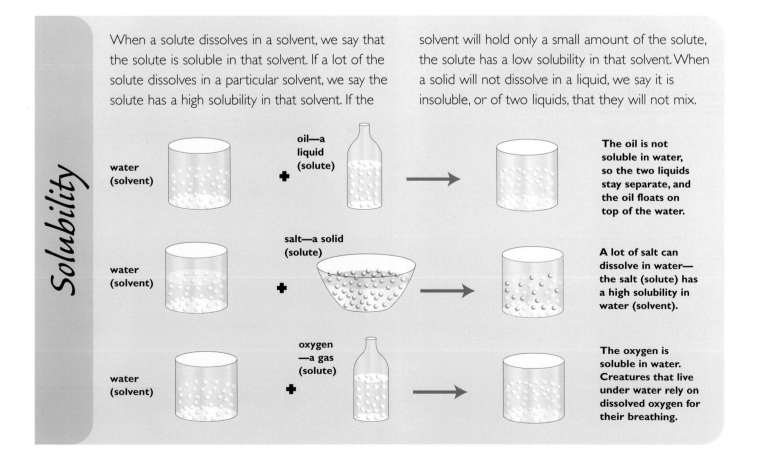

water (solvent) + oil—a liquid (solute) → The oil is not soluble in water, so the two liquids stay separate, and the oil floats on top of the water.

water (solvent) + salt—a solid (solute) → A lot of salt can dissolve in water—the salt (solute) has a high solubility in water (solvent).

water (solvent) + oxygen—a gas (solute) → The oxygen is soluble in water. Creatures that live under water rely on dissolved oxygen for their breathing.

Making a Solution

Goals

1. **Examine what happens when solids dissolve.**
2. **Find out how temperature affects solubility.**

What you will need:

- *measuring cup*
- *water*
- *mug and saucer*
- *notebook*
- *pen*
- *thermometer*
- *sugar*
- *teaspoon*
- *kettle*

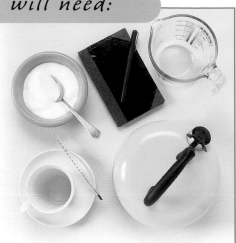

1 Fill a measuring cup to the 1 pint (500ml) mark with cold water from the tap. Use this water to fill the mug up to the brim very carefully. From the amount of water left in the cup, figure out how much water went into the mug. Write this figure down.

2 Carefully slide a thermometer into the water in the mug, and record the temperature.

Safety tip

Be very careful when handling hot liquids. It would be a good idea to get an adult to help you. Be careful not to spill any liquid; but if you do, wipe it up at once so that no one will slip on it—including you.

3 Carefully pour a spoonful of sugar into the water. Wait for the sugar to dissolve. Now add more spoonfuls of sugar, one at a time, taking care not to make the water splash over the edge of the mug.

Troubleshooting

What if I can't fill the mug to the rim without spilling?

You don't need to fill the mug to the very rim. Instead, you could use a felt-tip pen to make a mark on the inside of the mug (ask permission before marking up a good mug, or use a plastic beaker). Make a second mark just above the first mark. Fill the mug up to the bottom of the lower mark, and add sugar until the water level reaches the bottom of the upper mark.

4 When the mug overflows, write down the number of spoonfuls of sugar you added.

5 Now, repeat the experiment using the same amount of hot water.

Sticky solutions

Many glues work because they are solutions. The solvent makes the glue liquid so it can be spread onto the surfaces that are being glued together. Then it is left to set. The solvent then evaporates (turns to gas), leaving behind the solute, which is what holds together the two objects to be glued. Mixing flour and water is one way of making glue. The water is the solvent, and the flour is the solute.

FOLLOW-UP Making a solution

In order to get a wider range of results, you should repeat the activity using water at a variety of temperatures. You can then draw up a graph to show the relationship between temperature and solubility. You could also note how fast the sugar dissolves at different temperatures.

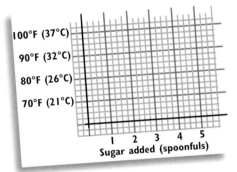

You may want to try the following simple experiment to demonstrate that a warm substance takes up more space than a cooler substance. With an adult present, melt a cube of butter or margarine in a pan or in the microwave. Pour the melted butter into a jar. Mark the level of the liquid butter on the outside of the jar with a washable marker. Or pour butter into the jar very carefully until it reaches the top. Now put the jar in the refrigerator until the butter has cooled down and formed a solid. You will find that the cold butter has shrunk below the level of the hot butter.

ANALYSIS Dissolving

In this activity you should have found that the higher the temperature of the water, the more solute will dissolve in it. When you raise the temperature of the water, the extra energy from the heat causes the molecules to move around more. As they move around, the spaces between the molecules get bigger, so more solute molecules can be fitted into the spaces between the solvent molecules.

This is also demonstrated in the follow-up activity with hot and cold butter. The heated, liquid butter takes up more space than the cooler, solid butter because the molecules in the hotter liquid are farther apart.

You may have found that there is a limit to the amount of solute that will dissolve in a solvent, no matter how long you waited. It is possible to have a solution that has the maximum amount of solute that the solvent will take at that temperature. It is called a saturated solution. If a hot, saturated solution is left to cool, the solvent molecules move close together and push the solute out of solution so it reappears as a solid. That is called precipitation. Precipitation also happens if some of the solvent evaporates. As it does so, there is no longer enough solvent for the dissolved solute, and the extra solute comes out of solution.

ACTIVITY 2
SEPARATING MIXTURES

If you have a bowl full of apples, oranges, and pears, you can separate them by picking out each kind of fruit and putting them into different piles. But how do you separate mixtures made from tiny particles?

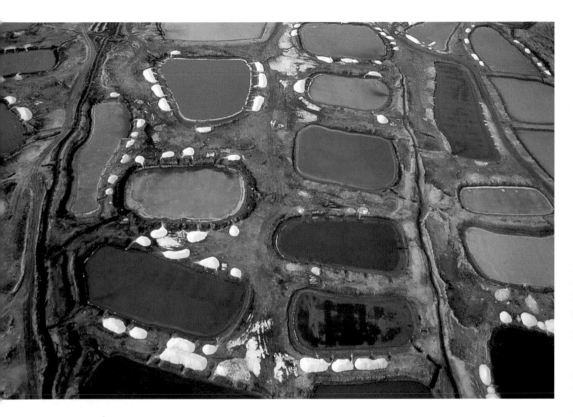

◀ **Salt pans in Egypt. Seawater is channeled into basins (pans) dug into the earth. The heat of the Sun makes the water evaporate, and workers rake the salt to the side in white heaps to dry out. Different salt-loving bacteria color the different pans in this picture.**

In Activity 1 (see pages 6 to 10) you dissolved a solute into a solvent to make a solution. But what if you want to separate two or more substances that are already in solution or a mixture of two solids and a liquid?

Scientists often need to separate mixtures in the laboratory in order to study just one of the substances. The method they choose depends on the type of mixture, the properties of the substances it contains, and which part of the mixture the scientists want to keep. For example, pasta does not dissolve in water, so you can use a strainer to separate pasta from its cooking water. This is filtration, and it is a good way to separate solids from liquids.

When making coffee, you add water to the grounds, then pour off and keep the liquid. This is called decanting.

When a solid is dissolved in a liquid, it can be separated out by waiting for the liquid to evaporate. Once there is not enough solvent to hold the solute in solution, the solute will become solid again. Another way to separate water from the solids dissolved in it is by boiling. The water turns to steam, which can then be collected and cooled so that it condenses back into water. This is called distillation and is how distilled water, which is pure water, is produced. In some very dry parts of the world fresh water for drinking is removed from salty seawater by a combination of distillation and filtration.

On the following pages you will have a chance to experiment with separating a solid, a dissolved solid, and a liquid.

Panning for Salt

Goals

1. **Test the solubility of substances in water.**
2. **Use decanting and evaporation to separate salt and sand.**

What you will need:

- *weighing scales*
- *2 ovenproof dishes*
- *tablespoon*
- *salt*
- *sand*
- *measuring cup*
- *water*
- *oven*
- *notebook*
- *pencil*

1 Zero the scale with one ovenproof dish already on it. Scoop up a tablespoon of salt, and pour it into the ovenproof dish. Write down the weight.

2 Repeat step 1 with a tablespoon of sand. Then add it to the salt.

3 With the help of an adult, boil some water, and add two cups of it to the sand and salt mixture. Stir until the salt dissolves. Let the mixture sit until the sand has settled to the bottom of the dish.

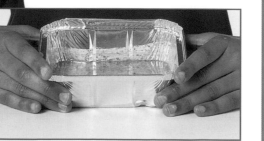

Safety tip

Always ask an adult to boil water for you and pour it into a measuring cup. Then pour the hot water very carefully into the dish.

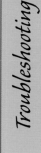

4 When all the sand has settled to the bottom, slowly pour the saltwater solution into the second ovenproof dish, taking care to leave the sand behind.

5 Put the two dishes into the oven, and ask an adult to turn it to a low heat (or, place the dishes outside on a sunny day). When all the water has evaporated, turn off the oven, and allow the dishes to cool completely. You should have one dish of dry sand and one dish of dry salt.

Troubleshooting

What if the water turns muddy when I stir it into the sand and salt mixture?

This means that the sand had dust mixed in with it. It would be best to wash some sand by mixing it with water and then pouring it off until the water is clear. Then dry the sand out in an oven, and start the experiment again.

Safety tip

Take great care when using the oven. If you need to look into the oven to see how the experiment is progressing, open the door, and wait for any steam to clear before moving your head near.

6 Weigh the sand and salt once again. Are the weights of each the same as they were at the start of the experiment?

FOLLOW-UP

Panning for salt

Repeat the experiment with different combinations of materials, one that will dissolve in water and one that won't. You could use sugar and sand or salt and gravel. Make sure the solid substance is heatproof. Carry out the experiment in exactly the same way. Are the results as you would expect them to be?

Always ask an adult for permission before heating anything or using hot water.

Note down the weights of the different ingredients (salt, sand, and sugar) at the beginning and then at the end of the experiment, using a table. Write a list of the ingredients down the left of the table and "Before" and "After" across the top. A table makes your results easier to read and compare.

Try another experiment. From the results of the experiment in Activity 1 (see pages 8 to 9) you should know how much salt you can add to a beaker of water so that all the salt dissolves. Mix up a beaker of salt and water, and leave it uncovered in a room for a few days. Measure the rate at which the water evaporates from the solution. Can you make the water evaporate faster?

ANALYSIS

Separating mixtures

In the activity you mixed together sand and salt, two solids, to form a mixture. When you added hot water to this mixture, you would have found that the salt went into solution, but that the sand did not dissolve.

Because sand is heavier than salt or water, over time the sand sank to the bottom of the dish. When you poured off the salt water, you were decanting it. Decantation is not a very precise method of separating a solid from a liquid. Because there is always a little bit of solid left, the smallest parts that are light enough to float in the liquid will get poured off as well.

When you left the saltwater solution to evaporate, you should have seen the salt come out of the solution and form a solid again—salt crystals. You probably found that the weight of the salt and sand after the experiment were not exactly the same as at the beginning of the experiment. Can you think of reasons for this?

One reason is that when you added water to the sand–salt mixture, some of the dissolved salt stuck to the sand grains and remained with the sand when the salt water was decanted. Similarly, some of the sand was probably decanted by accident and remained with the salt water. Examine the salt crystals with a magnifying glass. Can you see any sand grains mixed in with them that would prove this?

One thing that might affect your results is the fact that sand often comes mixed with a fair amount of water. To make sure that this does not cause problems, it might be a good idea to spread the sand on a baking sheet and heat it in the oven for an hour before you begin the experiment. As the water gets hot, it evaporates. Allow the sand to cool completely.

Sand that has been taken from a beach could also contain a small amount of salt. If you are using beach sand that has a lot of salt in it, you can remove most of the salt. Mix the sand with warm water so that the salt dissolves. Pour off most of the water, leaving the sand behind. Most of the salt will be poured away with the water. Now dry out the sand in the oven as before. There should be much less salt in the sand now. Builders do not use sand that has come straight from the beach because over time the salt that is mixed in with the sand will leach out. That means that it will slowly seep out of the mortar onto the surface of the building, creating ugly white stains.

DECANTING FOR GOLD

Decantation is used whenever substances with different densities need to be separated. Decanting was once one of the most common methods used to look for gold in rivers. It was called panning because big metal pans were used to scoop up a mixture of sand and water. The mixture was swirled around in the pan,

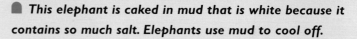
This elephant is caked in mud that is white because it contains so much salt. Elephants use mud to cool off.

and the heavy gold particles sank to the bottom. The unwanted muddy water was then decanted, leaving the gold flakes.

Evaporation is still used today in many parts of the world to separate salt from seawater. Salt is used in food preservation and is necessary for life, so people need a lot of salt.

Splitting mud

A mix of soil and water—mud—is easily separated. In a jar of very muddy water the soil particles spread evenly through the water. Once they settle to the bottom, the water can then be decanted off, though some mud particles still in the water will be poured off, and some water stays in the wet mud. Evaporation can be used to separate the rest of the water from the mud. Muddy water can also be filtered.

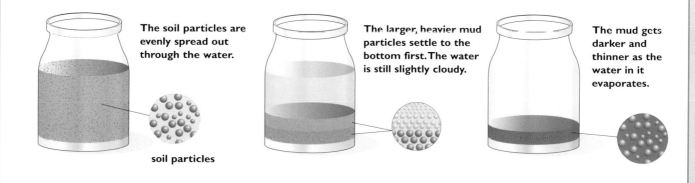

The soil particles are evenly spread out through the water.

soil particles

The larger, heavier mud particles settle to the bottom first. The water is still slightly cloudy.

The mud gets darker and thinner as the water in it evaporates.

ACTIVITY 3
CHROMATOGRAPHY

About 100 years ago Russian scientist Mikhail Tsvet (1872–1919) found a way of splitting the colors in plants. He called his technique chromatography, which simply means "color writing."

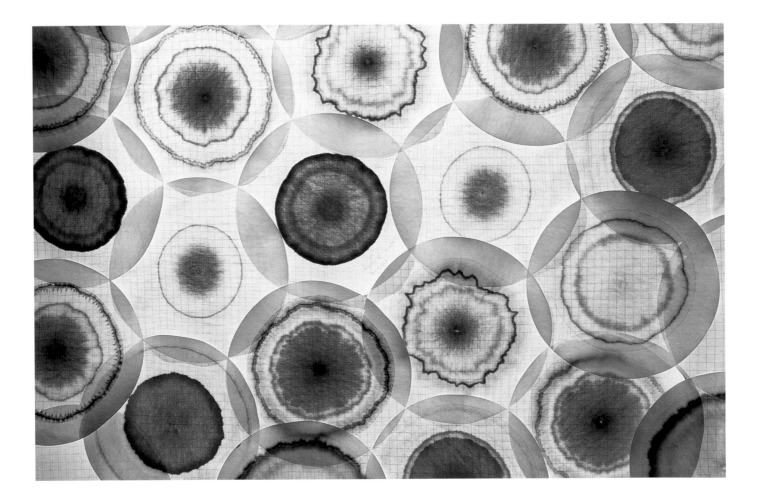

Scientists often need to test substances to find out what they are made of. If they are looking for a specific compound, they can do a test that gives a yes or no answer. Such tests include testing for sugar in urine for diabetes and pregnancy tests. There are many different substances in human urine, but each test is used to check the presence, or absence, of just one substance.

However, scientists sometimes want to get a complete list of all the chemicals in a substance. Chromatography is particularly good for this job

🔴 *Each paper circle, called a chromatogram, shows the different colors that make up some industrial dyes used for cloth. Scientists can tell what chemicals are in each color by the positions of the lines on the circles.*

because scientists can use it to separate even a complex mixture without knowing much about that mixture before starting work. The great advantage of chromatography is that it can be used to split a small amount of an unknown substance into its parts, and then each part can be tested.

There are two main types of chromatography: liquid chromatography and gas chromatography. Carrying out paper chromatography (a kind of liquid chromatography) is a good way of understanding how both types work. With a black washable felt-tipped pen, make a dot in the middle of a piece of plain, white paper towel that you have placed on a plate. Add a few drops of water, and watch the water move outward as the paper absorbs it. You will see the different colors in the ink separate and settle in a definite band as each one becomes too heavy to carry any farther. The lightest substances will travel farthest along the paper towel.

Chromatography consists of three basic parts: the substance to be tested (for example, the ink from the felt-tipped pen), the mobile phase (for example, the water) that moves the substance along the stationary phase (such as a paper towel). The lines created in paper chromatography can then be compared with the lines on other chromatograms, or a very pure sample of each chemical can be extracted from the paper for further tests.

USING CHROMATOGRAPHY

Gas chromatography uses a gas under pressure as the mobile phase, often helium or hydrogen. The stationary phase is either an absorbent material packed into a tube or a liquid coating on the inside of a tube. The police use gas chromatography to

Crimebusting

Chromatographers are scientists who work with law enforcement authorities such as the police and the FBI. Their work is important in catching criminals. Imagine that a group of people are suspected of being kidnappers. The authorities have a ransom note sent by the kidnappers and a pen belonging to the suspects. Forensic scientists can use chromatography to find out if the pen was the same as the one used to write the note. Ink is made from a mixture of chemicals, each of which will soak up to a different level on the paper. The ink from the pen is diluted with alcohol and allowed to soak into absorbent paper. The same thing is done with ink scraped from the ransom note. Chromatography will separate the different chemicals in the ink, leaving a distinctive series of lines. If the lines made by the two samples of ink match, the note was probably written with the same type of pen as the suspect's.

detect minute quantities of chemicals left behind on a bomb site after an explosion or to detect illegal steroids or drugs in urine.

The uses of liquid chromatography include analyzing the protein contents of a cell and measuring pollution in water. The mobile phase liquids have to be able to dissolve the substances to be analyzed without changing the molecules in any other way. Aside from paper (described above), the stationary phase can be a thin layer of absorbent material spread on glass. This is thin-layer chromatography, and it is commonly used to test for food additives.

For centuries people have added coloring to food to make it look more appetizing. Unfortunately, some of the colorings are harmful to people's health. Governments make laws that ban many food additives. The authorities regularly test food products with chromatography to make sure that manufacturers are not breaking the law.

◀ *A scientist carries out gas chromatography. She is using the complex equipment needed to detect the very small quantities of the substances being tested for.*

Separating Colors

Goals

1. **Demonstrate how chemicals can be separated.**
2. **Practice paper chromatography.**

What you will need:

- *white paper towel*
- *scissors*
- *glass measuring cup*
- *glass beaker or cup*
- *water*
- *2 water-based felt-tipped pens of different colors*
- *clothespin*

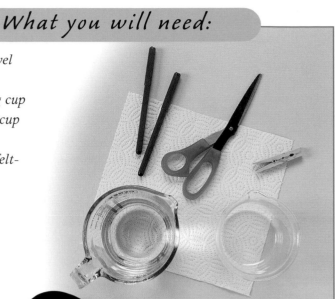

1 Cut a strip of white paper towel about 1 inch (2.5cm) wide and 4 inches (10cm) long.

2 Carefully pour about 1 inch (2.5cm) of water into the glass beaker or cup.

3 Put two dots of color, one with each felt-tipped pen, about 2 inches (5cm) from the end of the strip of paper towel. Make sure the colored dots are about the same size.

Colored candies

Brightly colored candies contain food coloring that is water soluble, so you can try crushing some candy into a dish and mixing it with warm water. Place a drop of this solution onto the paper towel, and wait to see the colors that separate out.

4 Use a clothespin to attach the piece of paper towel onto the edge of the beaker so that the marked end just touches the liquid.

Troubleshooting

What if the colors did not separate?

Try using a different color. Black is always made of several different colors and works very well. Brown is also a good color to use. Light colors, like yellow and pink, can be difficult to see and may give poor results. Also, make sure that you are using water-based ink. Only water-based dyes will dissolve in water.

5 Watch the water move up the paper towel—it should gradually take the chemicals that make up the colors of each dot with it. You may be surprised by the hidden colors that appear.

FOLLOW-UP Separating colors

Chromatography can be used to separate the colors in many materials. However, some of the chemicals that make up colors are not soluble (cannot be dissolved) in water and must be dissolved in other solvents before they can be separated using paper chromatography. Here is an experiment for separating the color compounds in flowers.

You will need:
brightly colored flower
clear vinegar
tablespoon
scissors
beaker or a glass bowl
paper towels
clothespin

2 Put all the flower pieces into the beaker, and add about one tablespoon of vinegar. Use the spoon to mash up the flower.

3 Soak the strip of paper towel in vinegar. Put one end into the flower pulp, and secure the strip over the beaker with the clothespin. The paper should hang straight down and just touch the flower and vinegar mix.

4 After about five minutes take the paper out of the bowl, and squeeze it between two paper towels to remove most of the vinegar.

5 At the top end of the paper, where it is dry, make a note of the type of flower you used and how long you allowed it to soak. You could also write down the date and time of the experiment so that the paper does not get mixed up with the others that you will eventually have.

6 Allow your chromatograms to dry, and then fasten them to a large sheet of paper so that you can compare the results. Look carefully to see if any of the lines from different flowers seem to match.

You can then draw up a table of results for the different flowers. Each column could have the name of the flower and the number of lines. Some lines might be very faint, to the point where you are not certain if there is a line or not. It might be best to use only the lines that you can definitely see clearly. Then you could note on your table the color of each line and its distance from the bottom of the paper.

1 Use clean scissors to cut a 2-inch (5cm) strip of paper towel. Then tear the flower into very small pieces, or cut it up with the scissors.

ANALYSIS
Chromatography

Most colors, like those in ink pens, are made up of several differently colored dyes mixed together. Each of these dyes is a different weight. The dyes in water-based pens dissolve in water, so when the water reached the spots of color, it dissolved the dyes and carried them up the paper towel as it moved up it. The dyes made of larger molecules rose more slowly and were separated from the colors made of smaller molecules first. In the end you should have had several bands of color, each representing a dye of a different weight.

The follow-up with the flowers worked the same way. In flowers the color usually comes from several different compounds mixed together. Most flowers, for example, contain chlorophyll, which is green. But in many flowers the green chlorophyll is "covered up" by other compounds of different colors. Some of

the chemicals in plants can be easily recognized as lines of color on the filter paper when you use paper chromatography. Two of the chemicals that give plants their green coloring are chlorophyll a and chlorophyll b. Chlorophyll a leaves a dark green line. The line for chlorophyll b is light green. Carotenoid, the chemical that gives carrots their orange color, leaves an orange line. Xanthophyl makes a yellow line. Many of these chemical compounds are not soluble in water, and that is why you need to use vinegar to dissolve them.

This method can be used to separate a wide variety of colored compounds. If you experimented with colored candies, you found that they also contain colored compounds that can be separated by weight. You might even have found that some of the colors in the candies were the same as those in the flowers.

Color in food

The Food and Drug Administration (FDA) is the government organization that controls which chemicals are allowed to be used in food, drugs, and cosmetics. The FDA allows only seven colorings to be used. If you have used chromatography to find the colorings used in candies, see if you can spot any of these colorings on the paper. You can also test food colorings that you buy in small bottles in food stores.

There are two blues. One is called Brilliant Blue (or number one blue), and it makes a bright blue color. It is used in drinks, jellies, and icing. The second blue is Indigotine (number two blue), and it produces a deep

blue color. It is used to color ice creams and cereals. Fast Green FCF, also called number three green, is greenish-blue and is used in ice cream, drinks, and candies.

Erythrosine, also called number three red, produces a bright red color and is used to color fruit and other products.

Allura Red AC, also called number 40 red, has a reddish-orange color and is used in puddings and dairy products.

Tartrazine, also called number five yellow, is used in candies, drinks, and ice cream. Sunset Yellow, also called number six yellow, is orange and is most commonly used to dye cereals and snack foods.

ACTIVITY 4
ALL ABOUT DENSITY

Matter can be arranged in many ways. Some of it is packed very tightly together, while in some substances it is arranged quite loosely. A substance's density is a measure of how tightly the matter is squeezed inside.

A satellite image of the Nile River flowing into the sea. The river's fresh water is not as dense as the salty seawater and floats on top of it.

a measure of how strongly gravity pulls an object toward Earth. A piece of steel weighing six pounds (2.7kg) on Earth only weighs one pound (0.4kg) on the Moon, where gravity is one-sixth as strong. However, the steel contains the same amount of matter and fills the same space on the Moon as it did on Earth, and therefore it has the same mass and density wherever it is.

FLOATING AROUND

Density is the mass of a substance compared with its volume. Mass is a measure of the amount of matter in an object, and volume is a measure of the space the object takes up. Which is more dense, steel or cork? A piece of steel is much heavier than a piece of cork of the same size. The cork and the steel take up the same amount of space, but the steel is heavier because it has more matter packed into it. Therefore, steel is denser than cork. It is important not to get confused between mass and weight when thinking about density. Weight is

An object's density affects how well it floats in liquid. Objects with lower densities than the liquid will float, while objects with higher densities than the liquid will sink. Liquids will also float on other, less-dense liquids. For example, the multicolored patterns that sometimes appear on the surface of puddles on roads are caused by a layer of oil floating on the water. The oil that drips out of cars and trucks into the puddles is less dense than the rain water. If the density of a liquid changes in some way, then that will affect how well solids and other liquids float on it.

There are two ways to change the density of a liquid. One is to increase its temperature. When a liquid is heated up, the atoms (tiny particles of matter) in the liquid move apart, and the liquid expands, taking up more space. Because its volume has increased, the liquid's density has decreased. Cooling the liquid will usually have the opposite effect, and the density will increase. Cooling liquids also turns them into solids, which generally are denser than their liquid forms.

DISSOLVING AND DENSITY

The density of a liquid increases when other substances dissolve in it. For example, when salt is dissolved in water, the mass of the salt is added to the mass of the water, but the volume of the liquid is more or less the same.

The Dead Sea (see page 27) is a large lake between Israel and Jordan that is filled with very salty water. The water is so dense that things that sink in fresh water float very easily—including people. See for yourself what changing the density of water can do by trying the activities on the next page.

Specific gravity

Winemakers use a hydrometer to measure the density of wine as it is being made (see below). That tells them the amount of sugar in the wine. Wines with a high density have more sugar in them. The more sugar there is, the more food the alcohol-making yeast has, and so the finished wine will have more alcohol in it. This measurement of the amount of sugar in wine (and beer) is called the specific gravity.

Weight, mass, and volume

You can measure an object in two ways: by its volume or by its mass. For example, you buy gasoline by volume (in gallons), that is, the amount of space it occupies. You buy apples by weight, however, which is a measure of how strongly gravity pulls the apples toward Earth. On Earth weight is effectively the same as mass; but when gravity is lower, such as on the Moon, the apples will weigh less.

The volume of a substance, such as water or metal, can be changed by adding heat or pressure. Nevertheless, the mass always stays the same.

Warming objects makes them expand; cooling causes them to contract. Pressure is a measure of a force in a particular area. Increasing the pressure on a substance squeezes it into a smaller volume.

When gravity pulls on an object, it creates a force called weight. The size of the force depends on the mass of the object. In the illustration below, all the cubes are the same size (have the same volume), but the lead, which is a very dense metal, weighs 13 times more than the wax and 56 times more than the balsa wood.

lead wax balsa wood

Sink or Swim

ACTIVITY

Goals

1. **Compare the density of fresh water and salt water.**
2. **Change the density of water.**

What you will need:

- 2 measuring cups
- 2 glass beakers
- water
- salt
- tablespoon
- 2 raw eggs

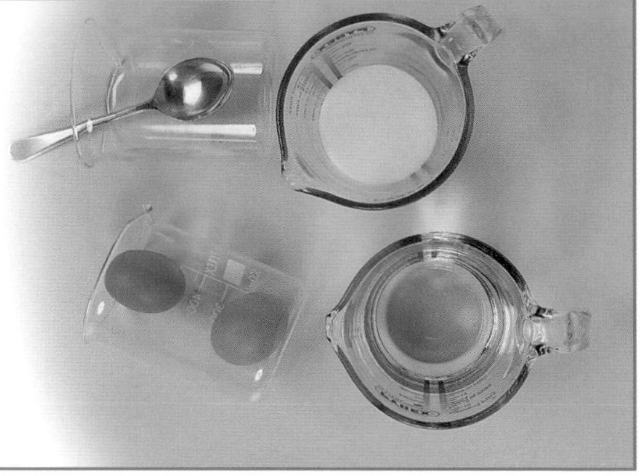

1 Fill two glass beakers with water up to the same level.

Measuring salt

Scientists can figure out how much salt there is dissolved in a stream or river by measuring the water's density using a device called a hydrometer. Salty water is denser than fresh water. Scientists need to know the salinity (salt content) of water to help them understand what lives in the water.

2 Pour some salt into one of the beakers.

3 Stir the salt in the water until it is totally dissolved.

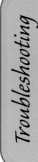

Troubleshooting

What if both of the eggs float at the same level?

Try adding more salt to the beaker of salt water. If you use just a little salt, you might not notice a difference in how the eggs float in each beaker.

Checking for rotten eggs

Measuring density can be used to check whether an egg is rotten or fresh. A fresh egg will sink in a cup of water that has two tablespoons of salt dissolved in it. If the egg floats, then it is probably rotten.

As eggs become rotten, they begin to produce a gas that gets trapped inside the shell. The trapped gas makes the egg less dense and more likely to float. If you crack open a rotten egg, the bad smell released is that gas escaping.

4 Drop a raw egg into each glass beaker, and see if they float.

FOLLOW-UP 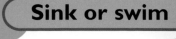 Sink or swim

You can measure the density of different liquids using your own hydrometer.

Making a hydrometer 1
What you will need:
clear plastic drinking straw
modeling clay
large glass of fresh water
permanent marker
salt
ruler

1 Seal one end of the plastic straw with modeling clay.

2 Put the straw in the glass of water. Use the permanent marker to mark how far up the straw the water reaches.

3 Remove the straw from the water.

4 Add about 1 ounce (25g) of salt to the water, and replace the straw. How far is the pen mark above water's surface now? Add more salt, and check again.

Making a hydrometer 2
What you will need:
large wine glass
maple syrup
glycerol
water (colored with dye)
olive oil
rubbing alcohol
metal screw
small plastic toy
cherry

1 Pour the maple syrup, then the glycerol, then the water (colored red here), then the olive oil, and last the rubbing alcohol into the glass. Pour slowly so the liquids do not mix together.

2 Gently drop the screw, plastic toy, and cherry into

the glass. Each of the objects should float at a different point inside the glass.

The liquids used in this experiment all have different densities and so form layers. Maple syrup is the most dense, and rubbing alcohol is the least dense liquid. The denser objects, such as the screw, float lower down in the glass in the denser liquid. The cherry and plastic toy are less dense, so they float in less dense liquids.

If you know the density of the objects you are putting in the hydrometer, you can make an estimate of how dense the liquids are. Remember, solid objects float in liquids that are denser than they are, but they sink through liquids that are less dense.

ANALYSIS

All about density

The salty water has more matter in it and is therefore denser than the fresh water. The egg should float in just the denser, salty water. In the follow-up the first hydrometer worked in a similar way to the first activity. The weighted straw floated higher up in denser salty water. The second hydrometer you made was useful for measuring the density of solids.

An object's density is often given as relative density. It is the difference between the object's own density and the density of pure water. Objects that float on water have a relative density of less than one. In other words, the object is lighter than the same volume of water.

Objects that sink in water have a relative density of more than one. They are heavier than the same volume of water.

Changes in density are easy to understand when you think about seawater. Seawater has a lot of salt and other minerals in it, making it more dense than fresh water. The salinity of ocean water changes around the world. Ships are designed to carry certain weights depending on the salinity of the water they are sailing through. If a ship takes on a full load at a seaport and then sails up a freshwater river, the ship will sink lower in the less dense water, and that could be dangerous.

The Dead Sea

The Dead Sea, bordering Israel and Jordan, is the lowest place on land. The surface of the Dead Sea is more than 1,300 feet (400m) below sea level and sinks by about 13 inches (33cm) a year. It is called the Dead Sea because it contains some of the saltiest water anywhere in the world, almost six times as salty as the ocean. No fish or water plants can live in the high salinity.

The salt in the Dead Sea is made up of dissolved minerals that are washed into the sea from the rivers and streams that run down from the surrounding mountains. However, because of the sea's unique climate, no water flows out of the Dead Sea.

Instead, a lot of the water evaporates (boils away) in the heat, leaving the mineral salts behind in the remaining water. The air above the sea is always very hot because the sea is at the bottom of a hole in the Earth's surface that is surrounded by mountains. Cooler air from the surrounding area just blows over the top of the Dead Sea's hot, still air, which never gets cooled.

The salts give the water a very high density—so high that people float in the Dead Sea without having to swim (see left). Unfortunately, the Dead Sea is emptying out because farmers are taking water from the rivers before it can flow into the lake.

ACTIVITY 5
TEMPERATURE AND PRESSURE

Gases are all around us—they make up the air we breathe. Unlike liquids and solids, gases are free to move around and fill any space. Understanding how they behave is important for predicting the weather.

■ *Clouds form and move around because of the relationship between temperature, pressure, and volume.*

Gases are made up of tiny units called molecules. They are the same molecules as in solids and liquids, but in gases the molecules are more free to move around. As the gas molecules move around a container, they cause a pushing force on the walls. This pushing force is called pressure. Pressure is caused by gas molecules bumping into each other and the molecules in the solid container. The more molecules there are in an area, the more often they bump into each other, and the higher the gas's pressure. Gas pressure is felt equally in all directions.

Volume, temperature, and pressure are very closely related to each other. Changing any one of them will cause changes in the others. Temperature is a measure of the amount of heat in a substance. When a gas is heated up inside a container with a fixed volume, the molecules in the gas begin to move around faster and bump into each other more often and at higher speeds, raising the pressure. If

The way gas behaves follows the ideal gas law, which describes how a gas's volume, pressure, and temperature change in relation to each other. The first diagram below shows the starting point, with temperature, pressure, and volume kept constant.

The second shows how pressure increases as volume decreases. The third illustrates that when gas is heated, its volume increases. The last diagram shows how both temperature and pressure will increase when a gas is squeezed into a smaller space.

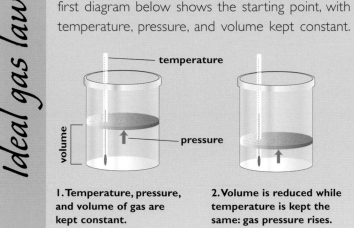

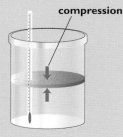

1. Temperature, pressure, and volume of gas are kept constant.

2. Volume is reduced while temperature is kept the same: gas pressure rises.

3. The temperature is raised, but pressure is kept constant: the gas expands.

4. The volume of gas is decreased (by squeezing, or compression): temperature and pressure both go up.

the volume of a gas is reduced, by squeezing the gas into a smaller space, for example, then the temperature and pressure of that gas will both rise. Pressure will rise because the molecules hit each other more often, and temperature goes up because the gas molecules are moving around more quickly.

WEATHER FACTORS

Earth's weather is caused by changes in the pressure, temperature, and volume of the air in the atmosphere. Air is a mixture of gases, mainly oxygen and nitrogen, and also contains water vapor (water in gas form), which forms clouds and falls as rain.

High in the atmosphere there are fewer gas molecules, so the pressure is much lower. Water on the surface of Earth is warmed and evaporates (turns to gas). As the water vapor rises through the atmosphere, its pressure decreases, so the vapor begins to cool down and eventually condenses (turns back into water) as tiny droplets on the surface of minute dust particles that are carried in the wind. These water-covered particles form clouds. If the air pressure or temperature goes down further, then all the water vapor in the air condenses and falls as rain. Low air pressure causes storms and unsettled, wet weather, while high air pressure usually brings calm air and clear skies.

Pressure cooking

The pressure cooker was invented by Denis Papin in 1679. It was first used as an industrial sterilizer, and only began to be used for cooking during World War II (1939–1945) because it saved time and fuel.

A pressure cooker is a sealed pot that, once heated up, is filled with high-pressure steam. The high pressure inside the pot keeps the rest of the water in the food from boiling. Instead, the water gets very hot, but still stays as a liquid and cooks the food very quickly and healthily. Soups, stews, risotto, pilaf, beans, puddings, and whole grains are great foods to cook in a pressure cooker.

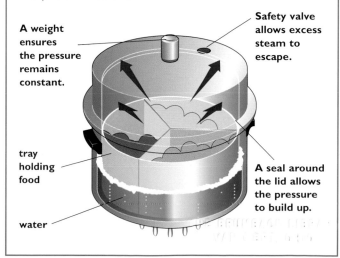

A weight ensures the pressure remains constant.

Safety valve allows excess steam to escape.

tray holding food

A seal around the lid allows the pressure to build up.

water

Cloud in a Jar

ACTIVITY

Goals

1. **Understand how volume, temperature, and pressure affect one another.**

2. **Use pressure to create a cloud in a jar.**

What you will need:

- *large, strong jar*
- *measuring cup*
- *water*
- *candle*
- *rubber glove*

1 Put about one-quarter of a cup of water into the bottom of the jar.

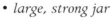

2 Turn the rubber glove inside out. Place a floating candle inside the jar. Ask an adult to light the candle. After a few seconds blow the candle out, and quickly stretch the glove around the neck of the jar so that it completely covers the neck of the jar.

3 Once the candle has gone out, put your hand inside the glove, and push your hand into the jar.

4 Carefully bend your fingers into a fist, and pull up while holding the jar steady with the other hand. Look into the jar as you do this. You should see a cloud form in the jar. Make sure the glove stays tight around the jar. The cloud should disappear when you stop pulling up.

5 Next, repeat the experiment, but this time place the glove over the jar while the candle is still burning, and wait for it to go out on its own. Once it's out, put your hand into the glove, and pull it out of the jar as before. Can you see any changes inside the jar this time?

Troubleshooting

What if the cloud does not appear in the jar in step 4?

It is very important that the seal between the glove and the jar is very tight. It is possible that you don't have a good seal, and that might be because the glove has a hole or because it is not fitting tightly enough. Try the other glove of the pair, and attach a rubber band around the rim of the jar.

Vapor trails

Water vapor is an invisible gas, but we can sometimes see it in the air as it turns from gas into a liquid. The vapor trails behind a jet airplane are just that. When a jet's fuel burns, it turns into hot gases, including water vapor. As the vapor is blasted out of the jet, it turns into water and ice as it meets the cold air outside. That forms the long, thin, cloudlike trails behind high-flying airplanes.

FOLLOW-UP Cloud in a jar

To explore the relationship between temperature, pressure, and volume of a gas, try changing the temperature of the air in the jar, and observe what happens. You can cool the air in the jar easily by placing it in the refrigerator after the candle has gone out. Heat the jar by putting it into a bowl of warm water.

You can also use a bicycle tire and air pump to explore the relationship between temperature and pressure. You will probably need a friend for this simple experiment.

First, have your friend work the pump so that the air is blowing over your hand. The air from the pump should feel colder than the air around you. Now feel the temperature of the bicycle tire. The bike should not have been ridden for a while, or the tires will be hot from rubbing against the road.

Next, pump air into the tire, and feel the temperature of the tire again. Then touch the pump. Do the tire and the pump feel colder or warmer than before? Try feeling the tire again ten minutes after the air has been added. How does it feel? Where has the extra heat energy gone?

■ *Pump air into the tire, and feel the change in its temperature.*

ANALYSIS

Temperature and pressure

During the main activity you should have seen a cloud form in the jar when the glove was pulled out. Pushing the glove back into the jar will make the cloud disappear again. Water molecules are present in the air in the form of invisible gas, or vapor. When you pull the glove up, you are forcing the air in the jar to expand. As the volume of the gas increases, it reduces the pressure, and the air in the jar also cools down.

When the molecules in water vapor cool and slow down, they can stick to each other more easily, so they begin to bunch up into tiny droplets. The particles of candle smoke in the jar help this process. The smoke particles provide a surface for the water vapor to form droplets on. When you push the glove back down, you increase the pressure in the jar, heating the air, and the cloud disappears as the droplets turn back into vapor. Clouds form in exactly the same way in the atmosphere, condensing in areas of low air pressure around particles of dust in the air.

Letting the candle burn inside the sealed jar increases the amount of water vapor inside. (Water vapor is produced by the burning wax.) With more of the air filled with vapor, a cloud should form more easily than before.

If you leave the glove hanging in the jar and warm up the jar, for example, by putting it in a bowl of warm water, you find that the glove begins to be pushed out of the jar. The extra heat energy in the air causes the molecules to air collide more often, increasing the pressure and making the gases fill a larger volume.

In the bicycle tire activity the pump and tire will feel warmer after pumping. The pump works by squeezing air out through a nozzle. That raises the pressure and the temperature of the air. As the pump forces air into the tire, the pressure inside also increases, since the tire's valve only lets air in and not out again. This rise in pressure makes the tire warmer.

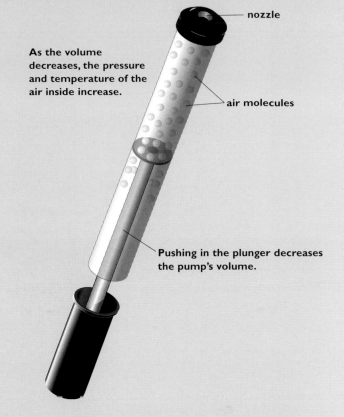

nozzle

As the volume decreases, the pressure and temperature of the air inside increase.

air molecules

Pushing in the plunger decreases the pump's volume.

🔲 *A bicycle pump works by reducing the volume of a gas (by compression), increasing its pressure, and sending it shooting out the end of the pump.*

Refrigerator

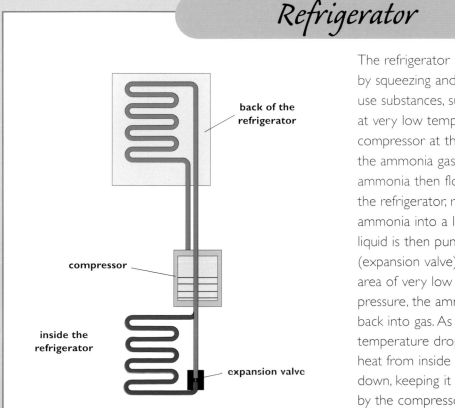

back of the refrigerator

compressor

inside the refrigerator

expansion valve

The refrigerator in your kitchen keeps your food cold by squeezing and expanding a gas inside it. Refrigerators use substances, such as ammonia, which turn into gases at very low temperatures (−27°F; −32°C). A compressor at the bottom of the refrigerator squeezes the ammonia gas, so it heats up under pressure. The ammonia then flows through the coils on the back of the refrigerator, releasing the heat and turning the ammonia into a liquid. The high-pressure ammonia liquid is then pumped through a small nozzle (expansion valve). On the other side of the nozzle is an area of very low pressure. Once in the area of low pressure, the ammonia immediately expands and turns back into gas. As it does this, the ammonia's temperature drops to −27°F. The cold gas removes the heat from inside the refrigerator, which cools the food down, keeping it fresh. The cold gas is then sucked up by the compressor, and the cycle repeats.

ACTIVITY 6
GAS EXPANSION

Gases are substances with no fixed volume or shape. They consist of moving particles that expand as they move from areas of high concentration to areas of low concentration.

Chemical reactions are happening all the time. They occur when atoms or molecules combine to form new chemical substances. Some reactions take hundreds or even thousands of years, while others are over in a fraction of a second. The rate of reaction measures how quickly the reaction takes place. A low rate means the atoms and molecules combine slower than in a reaction with a high rate.

Collision theory is a useful way of describing how quickly or slowly reactions occur. This theory suggests that reactions take place as a result of collisions between atoms and molecules. The more

Champagne is fizzy because it contains carbon dioxide gas. If you shake a bottle of champagne, the gas expands inside and exerts pressure on the cork. Sometimes the pressure is enough to blow the cork out of the bottle.

atoms and molecules there are in a given space, the higher the number of collisions there are, and the faster the rate of reaction.

Several factors affect the rate of a chemical reaction. The first is the concentration of reactants, or substances involved in the reaction. A high concentration means that more atoms and molecules are present in a given volume. This means that the particles are more likely to collide with one another, and the reaction will be faster.

Temperature also affects the rate of reaction. Atoms and molecules are constantly moving. At higher temperatures atoms and molecules have more energy and move around a lot more. That makes them more likely to collide and react.

Pressure also affects the rate of chemical reactions. When you increase the pressure, the atoms and molecules have less space. That means they are more likely to collide with one another.

MEASURING REACTION RATES

It is hard to measure the rate of some reactions because it is not always obvious the reaction is occurring. When two chemicals react to produce a gas, it is sometimes easier to measure the rate of reaction because the expansion of the gas creates pressure. If enough gas is produced in the reaction, the pressure created can push other gases, liquids, and even solids out of the way. That is called displacement. Displacement is used in devices such as fire extinguishers (see the diagram at right).

The activity on the following pages will show you how to measure the rate of a chemical reaction by observing the displacement of water by a gas.

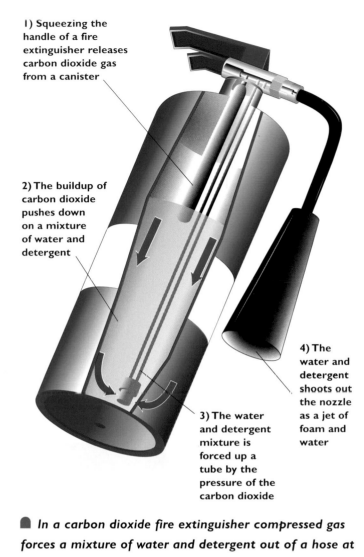

1) Squeezing the handle of a fire extinguisher releases carbon dioxide gas from a canister

2) The buildup of carbon dioxide pushes down on a mixture of water and detergent

3) The water and detergent mixture is forced up a tube by the pressure of the carbon dioxide

4) The water and detergent shoots out the nozzle as a jet of foam and water

In a carbon dioxide fire extinguisher compressed gas forces a mixture of water and detergent out of a hose at high pressure.

Gas behavior

Gases spread out, or expand, to fill up any available space. As they expand, the gases always move from areas of high concentration, where there are more particles, to areas of low concentration, where there are fewer particles. This process is called diffusion. In an enclosed space gases continue to diffuse until they are evenly distributed within that space. The process of diffusion continues because the particles that make up the gases try to keep the same distance from one another.

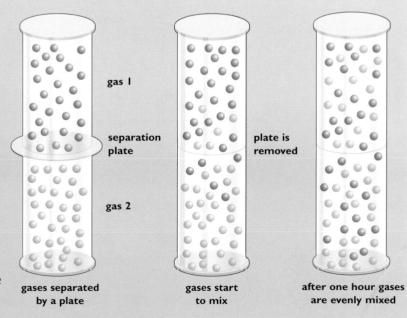

gas 1

separation plate

gas 2

plate is removed

gases separated by a plate

gases start to mix

after one hour gases are evenly mixed

ACTIVITY

Gas Bottle

Goals

1. **Measure the rate of a chemical reaction.**
2. **Study the rate of gas expansion.**

What you will need:

- *small glass jar with its lid*
- *large glass jar with its lid*
- *3 ft (1 m) of plastic tubing*
- *modeling clay*
- *screw cap from a large plastic drink bottle*
- *eyedropper*
- *measuring cup*
- *Alka-Seltzer™ tablets*
- *thermometer*

1 Ask an adult to help you pierce holes in the lids of the glass jars. You will need to make one hole in the small jar's lid and two holes in the large jar's lid. Each hole must be big enough to fit the plastic tubing inside.

2 Cut the plastic tubing in half. Push one length of tubing a little way into the hole in the small lid. Use modeling clay to seal around the hole and tubing.

3 Press a small piece of clay onto the bottom of the screw cap. Pop the cap into the jar and push on it to stick the clay to the bottom of the jar.

4 Use an eyedropper to fill the screw cap with water. Place an Alka-Seltzer™ tablet next to the cap in the jar. Do not spill water onto the tablet.

5 Carefully screw the lid onto the small jar. Push the free end of the plastic tubing into one of the holes in the large lid. Seal the hole and tubing with modeling clay. Then take the second piece of tubing, and push it a little way into the second hole in the large lid. Seal around the hole as before.

6 Fill the large glass jar two-thirds full of water, and screw the lid on tightly. Now you need to siphon off some of the water from the large jar into the measuring cup. You can do that by gently sucking on the end of the second piece of tubing until you feel water on your tongue. When this happens, quickly insert the end of the plastic tubing into the measuring cup. The water level will gradually rise up the measuring cup. Raise the cup until the water level stops rising. At this stage water will fill the plastic tubing leading from the second jar to the measuring cup. Record the water level in the measuring cup. Then make a note of the temperature in the room.

Troubleshooting

What should I do if the water level does not change?
Gas released by the Alka-Seltzer™ tablet might be escaping through a gap where you sealed the holes and tubing with modeling clay. Try sealing the holes with more clay and doing the experiment again.

Acid indigestion

Alka-Seltzer™ and similar over-the-counter medicines are used for indigestion. Substances in the stomach help digest food, but sometimes the chemical balance is upset. The stomach becomes too acidic, and the chemicals irritate the stomach wall, causing indigestion. Indigestion remedies contain an alkali to neutralize the acid in the stomach. Adding an alkali to an acid in this way produces harmless salts, but it also releases carbon dioxide. As a result, many people burp after taking these remedies.

7 Now you are ready to start the experiment. Tilt the small jar so that the water in the screw cap spills over onto the Alka-Seltzer™ tablet. Record the level of water in the measuring cup at regular intervals. How much water is displaced from the large jar? How quickly is the water displaced?

FOLLOW-UP Gas bottle

Record the level of water in the measuring cup every five seconds. Compile your results into a table. The volume of water that is displaced is equal to the amount of carbon dioxide gas released.

Change the temperature of the reaction by placing the small jar in a bowl of warm water or ice. Before you start, measure the temperature in the bowl. Wait a few minutes before you start. It will take a few minutes for the temperature of the water to

affect the temperature of the jar and its contents. You can also try changing the rate of the reaction by changing the concentration of

the Alka-Seltzer™. Use two tablets, and then repeat the experiment with half a tablet.

Draw a graph of the amount of gas produced (as measured by the rising water) against time for each temperature. Do the same for the experiments with more or fewer tablets.

The displacement of water is due to the expansion of gas. The more gas there is, the more water is moved. Changing the temperature or the water or concentration of Alka-Seltzer™ changes the rate of reaction.

ANALYSIS

Gas expansion

In this experiment you first created a chemical reaction that produced a gas, then noted the speed at which the gas expanded to examine the rate of the reaction. The faster the reaction, the faster the gas expanded.

Alka-Seltzer™ contains two chemicals: sodium bicarbonate (an alkali) and citric acid (an acid). When mixed with water, the chemicals combine to produce carbon dioxide gas. The gas filled the small jar and then passed through the plastic tubing. As the gas expanded, its pressure increased. The gas

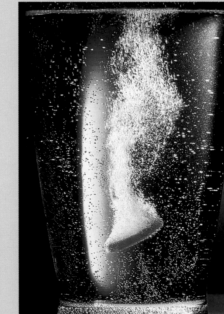

■ *The fizz when adding water to Alka-Seltzer™ is carbon dioxide gas.*

moved into the second jar, where the pressure of the gas pushed on the water in the large jar, forcing it up the second tube and out into the measuring jug.

You should have found that the higher the temperature, the faster the reaction occurred. Similarly, the more Alka-Seltzer™ tablets you used, the more gas was produced, and more water was displaced.

At the start of the experiment you siphoned water into the plastic tubing. That was necessary because any air trapped in the tubing would apply pressure on the water in the large jar and affect the results.

ACTIVITY 7
REDOX REACTIONS

As you breathe air into your lungs, you are fueling a redox reaction. The oxygen you take in is used in respiration, which is the reaction that generates the energy to keep you alive.

Redox reactions are a type of chemical reaction. Redox is short for reduction and oxidation reaction. Many redox reactions are very familiar: the way that apple flesh turns brown in air, burning, respiration (using oxygen to generate energy for life processes), and photosynthesis (the way that plants make food from water and carbon dioxide using the energy of sunlight).

Redox reactions take place in two parts. The part in which oxygen is gained is called oxidation, and the part in which oxygen is lost is called reduction. Another way of studying redox reactions is by looking at where the electrons have been gained or lost. Oxygen easily takes electrons, so the substance that has been oxidized loses electrons. The oxygen, having gained electrons, is said to have been reduced. The mnemonic OIL RIG makes this easier to remember. It stands for *oxidation is loss* (of electrons), *reduction is gain* (of electrons).

Apple and avocado slices turn brown in air because the oxygen in the air is combining with a substance in the fruit to make a brown oxide. Burning (often called combustion) describes a

🔴 *For a fire to burn, it needs oxygen, fuel, and a high temperature. A plane drops fire retardant to take the oxygen out of the "fire triangle."*

reaction in which a substance combines with oxygen to form an oxide and gives off heat at the same time. Most fuels (such as wood or gasoline) contain compounds of carbon and hydrogen. When the fuel burns, the carbon is oxidized to carbon dioxide, and the hydrogen is oxidized to water. The oxygen gains electrons and is therefore reduced.

Respiration is a slow form of combustion during which carbon and hydrogen atoms in glucose are oxidized to form carbon dioxide and water (with an accompanying release of energy, which is the point of the reaction).

Photosynthesis is the opposite of respiration, since carbon dioxide and water are reduced to glucose, and some oxygen is oxidized (loses electrons). In photosynthesis water carried into the plant by its roots arrives at the leaves. The leaves have in them a chemical called chlorophyll, which is what makes them green. Chlorophyll uses the energy of sunlight to split water molecules into their component parts of oxygen and hydrogen. The atoms of hydrogen and oxygen then react with carbon dioxide to make glucose and oxygen.

Testing Photosynthesis

Goals

1. **Examine the rate at which a redox reaction takes place.**

What you will need:

- *tall drinking glass*
- *pondweed*
- *water*
- *saucer or bowl*
- *marker pens*
- *ruler*
- *measuring cup*

1 Put a strand of the pondweed into the glass, and fill the glass up to the brim with water.

2 Put the saucer over the top of the glass, and quickly turn the glass and saucer upside down while holding them in place. A small amount of water will run out of the glass.

3 Quickly pour a small amount of water into the saucer. This will keep water from running out of the glass.

④ Look at the top of the glass. A small amount of air should be trapped there. Mark the level of the air with a marker pen.

Troubleshooting

What if all the water pours out of the glass when I tip it up?

The glass may have an uneven rim, or the saucer may have an uneven base. Try different glass and saucer pairs until you get a good fit.

You also need a very steady hand when you are doing the trick of tipping it over. You may have to practice a few times before you get it absolutely right.

⑤ Now leave the glass and saucer on a sunny windowsill for a few hours. Mark the water level again at a set time interval, such as one hour.

Photosynthesis under water

As it travels through water, some of the energy in sunlight is lost. So different seaweeds have different proportions of chlorophyll types to make use of the sunlight reaching them. Chlorophyll a and b occur in most algae; chlorophyll c occurs in brown algae; which lives at greater depths; and chlorophyll d occurs in red algae.

⑥ Measure the distance between two marks. Continue to mark the glass at regular intervals. You could also try putting the plant in direct sunlight to see what effect that would have on the rate of reaction. You might have to move the plant to catch the sun, so be aware of any changes in temperature in the new location.

FOLLOW-UP   Testing photosynthesis

When you examine the plant at regular intervals over the course of a day, note what is happening inside the jar, and describe it in your notebook. Look for any bubbles on the plant and in the glass, and describe how they move.

Measure the level of the water in the glass, and note it down also. You can then draw a graph of the level of the water against time. You can use the level of either the water in the glass or the water in the dish since the water in the dish will be forced out by the buildup of gas in the top of the glass. Use whichever of the results give the largest figures, because they will be easier to plot on a graph.

There might be one small disadvantage to using the results for the water level in the dish. Some of the water from the dish will evaporate as it is exposed to the air, and that will make the readings wrong. On the other hand, the water in the glass is sealed and cannot evaporate so will produce a more accurate reading.

Repeat the experiment by placing the plant in a dark cupboard. Is less air produced? You can also try the experiment at different temperatures.

Compare the results from all the different experiments. What difference do darkness, sunlight, and temperature make to the production of gas?

Ask an adult to help you test the gas that the plant has made really is oxygen. Take the glass and dish to a sink, and carefully tilt the glass so that the water can flow slowly out. This must be done as gently as possible so that the gas in the top of the glass is not disturbed. Ask the adult to strike a long cook's match. Keeping the glass upside down, carefully put the flame into the gas at the top of the glass. What happens to the flame? The flame should burn better in the gas. That is because it is oxygen—the gas in air— that allows things to burn.

ANALYSIS   Redox reactions

The amount of oxygen produced in the activity will vary. If the plant is placed in direct, strong sunlight, it will produce more oxygen. That is because sunlight supplies the energy that is needed by the chlorophyll in the plant for photosynthesis to happen. Without sunlight the reaction will not happen. That is how Earth obtains energy from the Sun.

The temperature that the experiment is carried out in will also make a difference. As with any chemical reaction, the heat energy causes molecules to move around more so that they collide more often. So, the higher the temperature of the room and the water, the more oxygen the plant will produce in any given time. Eventually, if the temperature gets too high, the cells of the plant and the substances inside them will become damaged, and that will affect the production of oxygen.

If the temperature is reduced, oxygen production will slow down because reactions tend to slow down as temperatures decrease. When the temperature drops to the freezing point, the plant has another problem: The water in the plant turns to ice crystals. Because ice crystals take up more space than liquid water, they will break and kill the plant cells.

Plants and all other organisms strike a fine balance when it comes to using the atmosphere. All living organisms except plants take oxygen from the air and replace it with carbon dioxide. Plants and algae do the opposite, taking in carbon dioxide and giving out oxygen as long as they are in sunlight. Plants use up oxygen at night. Overall though, they give off more oxygen than they absorb. Plants and other organisms could not live without one another.

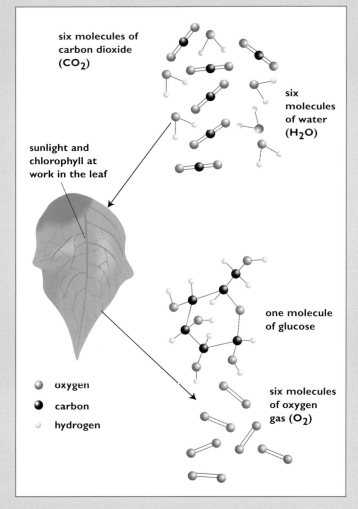

six molecules of carbon dioxide (CO_2)

six molecules of water (H_2O)

sunlight and chlorophyll at work in the leaf

one molecule of glucose

six molecules of oxygen gas (O_2)

○ oxygen
● carbon
○ hydrogen

▶ *Photosynthesis takes place inside green leaves in the presence of sunlight. Water and carbon dioxide are recombined to make glucose and oxygen.*

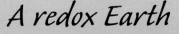

A redox Earth

You can see how important redox reactions are when you realize Earth's crust is the result of a redox reaction between the metal core and the oxygen in the surrounding atmosphere. Most of Earth's crust is made up of metal oxides, and even water is an oxide of hydrogen. Most chemical reactions happen because the reactants are more reactive than the results of the reactions. Oxygen is a very reactive element. Although it is not as abundant in the atmosphere as nitrogen, the high reactivity of oxygen explains why so many of the

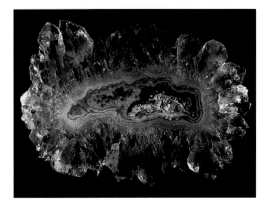

■ *The purple form of quartz (amethyst) is silicon dioxide, a very common mineral.*

compounds in the Earth's crust are oxides.

Many of the reactions in industrial metal extraction are redox reactions, using oxides as raw materials. The production of iron is a good example. Iron oxide is heated with carbon. The iron oxide is reduced to iron, while the carbon is oxidized to carbon dioxide. Because many oxides are so stable, many of these redox reactions have to be helped along by very high temperatures or a catalyst (a chemical that speeds up a reaction).

ACTIVITY 8
MAGIC MIXTURES

Did you know that a solid object is mostly empty space? Between the atoms and molecules in matter are billions of tiny gaps. You can make substances disappear into these gaps by mixing things together.

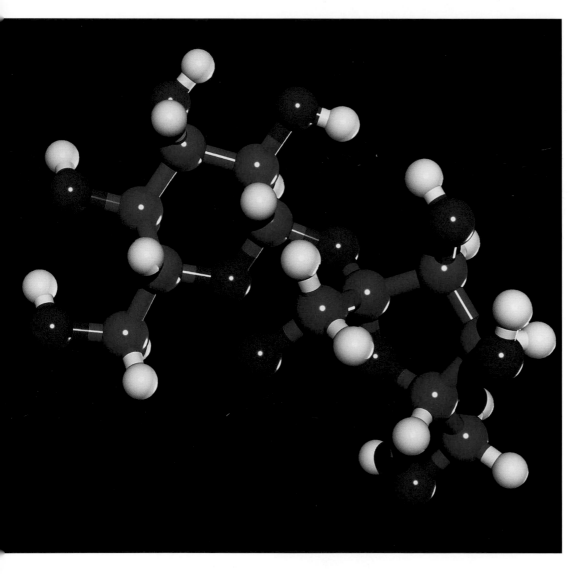

This is a computer-generated image of a molecule of the sugar agarose. In between the atoms is empty space.

30 football fields. Apart from the nucleus and electron, the whole model would be empty space.

This activity is all about the spaces between molecules. It's tempting to think that the molecules in an object are packed tightly together, but in fact there is often lots of space between them. Even in something solid, like a table, there is space between the molecules. Liquids, such as oil and water, have even more space between their molecules, and that allows the molecules to move around freely. Gases have more space still.

Nothing in the universe is as solid as it looks. There are spaces between the molecules that make up substances, spaces between the atoms that form molecules, and even spaces inside atoms. If you made a scale model of a hydrogen atom, using a pea for the nucleus and a fleck of dust for the electron, your model would be wider than the length of

One way to imagine the spaces between molecules is to think of a bucket filled to the top with stones. Although the bucket looks full, you can pour in sand—the sand flows into the spaces between the stones. But the bucket still wouldn't really be full. You could pour water in as well, and the water would fill the gaps between the sand

In the mix

The molecules in a liquid move around freely because there are large spaces between them. When two different liquids mix together to form a solution, the different molecules mingle evenly together. Because the different molecules fit between each other's gaps, the mixture takes up less space than the total space taken up by the separate liquids.

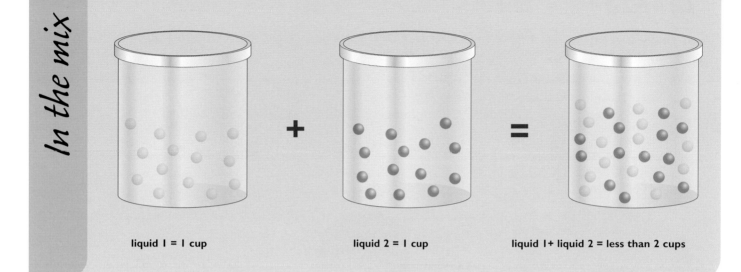

liquid 1 = 1 cup

liquid 2 = 1 cup

liquid 1 + liquid 2 = less than 2 cups

grains. Likewise, when you stir sugar into a cup of coffee, the level in the cup hardly rises. The water molecules and the sugar molecules fit between each other easily without taking up much extra space.

When two substances mix together completely, like sugar in hot coffee, they form what we call a solution. We say the sugar dissolves as it disappears into the coffee. Most solutions are made from water and a solid, but lots of different substances can mix to form a solution. Carbon dioxide gas, for example, will dissolve in water when the water is under pressure. One example of this solution is fizzy soda. When you release the pressure in a soda bottle by taking the top off, bubbles of carbon dioxide are released. Liquids can also dissolve in other liquids. For example, ethanol and water form a solution.

On the next page you can find out how to make a solution from two different liquids: water and rubbing alcohol (isopropyl alcohol). When you mix these two together, you should find that the mixture takes up less space than the total space taken up by the separate ingredients. That is because the molecules of one liquid will fit into gaps between molecules of the other, just as sand fits into the gaps in a bucket full of stones.

Buckyballs

Many substances have spaces between their molecules, but a few actually have spaces inside the molecules. One is buckminsterfullerene, an amazing chemical that was discovered in 1985. Molecules of buckminsterfullerene are called "buckyballs" and are made of 60 carbon atoms joined in the shape of a soccer ball. Because the hollow centers can hold other atoms, buckyballs might one day prove very useful. However, despite years of work, scientists are still searching for the best way to use them.

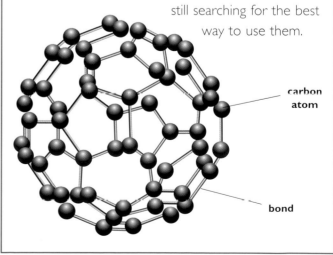

carbon atom

bond

ACTIVITY

Disappearing Trick

Goals

1. **Make a solution from two liquids.**
2. **Find out how substances differ at the molecular level.**

What you will need:

- *2 tall, straight glasses*
- *washable marker pen*
- *measuring cup*
- *rubbing alcohol (isopropyl alcohol)*
- *felt-tipped pens*
- *water*

1 Use a washable marker to make a mark on the outside of the glass about a third of the way up. Fill the glass with water up to the bottom of the mark.

2 Pour the water out of the first glass and into the second glass.

3 Pour more water into the first glass up to the bottom of the mark again, and again pour the water into the second glass.

4 Use the pen to mark the water level on the outside of the second glass. This is the amount of two measures of water from the first glass. Now empty the second glass, and make sure you keep the mark on it.

Supercool cars

The size of the gaps between molecules in a liquid depends on how warm the liquid is. If you cool a liquid down, the liquid shrinks. Racing cars make use of this principle. To keep the fuel tank as small as possible, they use fuel that is freezing cold, so that it takes up less space inside the tank.

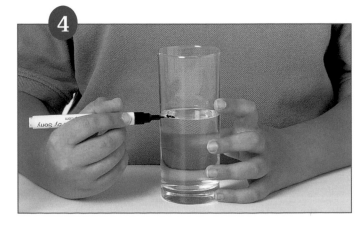

5 Once again, fill the first glass up to the bottom of the mark with water. Empty this water into the second glass, as before.

6 Now fill the first glass to the bottom of the mark with rubbing alcohol.

7 Pour the rubbing alcohol into the second glass (with the water in it).

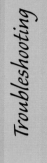

Safety tip

Rubbing alcohol is a poisonous substance. Do not drink it or get it near your eyes or nose. Have an adult present whenever you are using rubbing alcohol. It is safe to touch.

8 Notice the level of the liquid in the second glass. Is it above or below the mark from two glasses of water? How far above or below the mark is it?

FOLLOW-UP

Disappearing trick

It is a good idea to repeat the activity using measuring cups so that you can get a more accurate measurement of exactly how much the mixture shrank.

Try using other liquids instead of rubbing alcohol. You could use vinegar, methanol, turpentine, vegetable oil, orange juice, or milk. Since some of these substances are dangerous chemicals, it is important to always have an adult present when you try this activity.

Do all the mixtures take up less space than the separate parts? Can you guess why or why not?

▶ *Try using other kinds of liquids, but make sure you first ask an adult which liquids are safe to use.*

◀ **Draw a graph of all the different mixtures to record how much they shrank when mixed with water.**

Graph:
Amount final mixture shrunk in inches

1¼
1
½
¼
0

alcohol   bleach   vinegar   turpentine

Liquid used with water

ANALYSIS

Magic mixtures

In this activity the two liquids appeared to magically shrink when you poured them together to make a solution. Of course, there was nothing magic about it. The total volume of the solution was less than the combined volumes of the liquids because the molecules in the solution fitted more closely together. The "trick" only works if the molecules in the two liquids are a different size—so the small molecules can fit into the gaps between the big ones.

The liquids that shrink to the lowest level when mixed with water are the ones with the biggest molecules. Water molecules are made from just two atoms of hydrogen and one of oxygen, so they are quite small. This allows them to fit easily into the gaps between mole-

Paint is an emulsion of chemical pigments (color), and oil or water.

colloids. Milk, for example, is an emulsion of oil droplets in water. Mayonnaise is an emulsion made from oil, an acid such as vinegar or lemon, and egg yolk. The egg yolk is called an emulsifier because it keeps the mixture from separating. Some types of paint are also made of different liquids mixed together in an emulsion.

Water and rubbing alcohol dissolve together easily because their molecules attract each other. You can mix them in any proportion, and they will always dissolve completely. Liquids that form solutions easily are called solvents. They are useful for cleaning up all sorts of dirt and grease because they make other substances dissolve easily.

cules of other liquids. The bigger the molecules of the other liquid, the more room there is for the water molecules. In the follow-up you may have found that certain liquids made the solution shrink more than others. They were the liquids with the largest molecules.

But you probably found that the experiment didn't always work. If you mixed water with orange juice or vinegar, your solution would not have shrunk at all. That's because these liquids are mostly water, so you were really mixing water with water. If you used oil, you would have found that the oil sat on top of the water instead of mixing into it, and the volume would not have changed.

Liquids that dissolve into each other are called miscible, while those that don't mix are immiscible. Immiscible liquids cannot form a solution, but they can be mixed in other ways. If you shake a mixture of oil and water for long enough, the oil will break up into thousands of tiny droplets that hang in the water. That is called a suspension. Eventually, the droplets float to the surface and join together, separating the suspension into layers of oil and water.

Some suspensions can stay mixed together permanently, and they are called emulsions or

Colored glass is an emulsion of glass and pigment.

ACTIVITY 9
BUBBLE SCIENCE

Bubbles are made mainly of water molecules held together by tiny amounts of soap or detergent. You can find out a lot about water molecules if you look closely at the surface of a bubble.

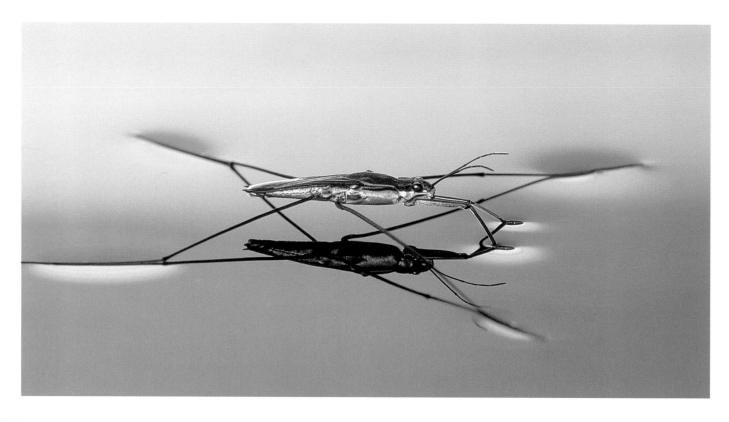

🔴 *The tension at the surface of a body of water is one reason that insects, such as pond skaters like this one, can walk across the water.*

Next time you drink a glass of water, look closely at the surface of the water, you will see that it looks a bit like a tight elastic sheet stretched over the liquid. Fill the glass to the brim, and look at the surface of the water from the side. You should be able to see that the water in the middle of the glass is slightly higher than at the sides.

The molecules in a glass of water are constantly moving. Collisions produce weak attractive forces that hold the water molecules together. Imagine a molecule in the center of the glass. Weak forces are constantly being formed as molecules collide with their neighbors in all directions. Now imagine a molecule at the surface of the water. It will be attracted to all the other water molecules around it,

both to the sides and below. There are no water molecules above, so there are no attractive forces acting above the molecule. This pulls the molecules at the surface tighter together—it is called a state of tension. The water in the middle is higher than the surface of the water at the sides because the force of attraction across the water's surface is stronger than the force of gravity. When water is not in a container, the force of attraction pulls it into a round shape. So, raindrops would be round if the force of gravity did not flatten them slightly.

Pulling together

Molecules of water attract one another—they pull each other equally in all directions. The water molecules on the surface of a glass of water can only be pulled by the molecules underneath. This force of attraction, termed surface tension, pulls it into a tight film. The tension is strong enough to allow insects to walk on the water's surface.

Even if the water is not held in a container, the force of attraction between the molecules is still very strong. In fact, it is strong enough to pull the water together into a rounded shape. Gravity then flattens the drop slightly.

Molecules on the surface of a glass of water are pulled by molecules underneath and to each side.

Droplets of water are not teardrop shaped, as many people think. Instead, they are slightly flattened spheres. The first drop (above right) is teardrop shaped since it is still attached to the faucet.

If you dunk a wire hoop into soapy water and gently pull it out, a film of water will stretch out and form a flat surface across the hoop. The attraction between the water molecules pulls them into the shape that fills the hoop but has the smallest possible surface area—a flat circle. If you bend the wire into a complex shape, dunk it into the solution, and then pull it out, a film forms again. Once again, the film that forms in the space between the wires will occupy the smallest possible surface area.

Calling these bubbles soap bubbles is a bit misleading. The bubbles are mostly made of water mixed with just a tiny amount of soap. In fact, the soap is only added to lower the surface tension of the water, making the water molecules stretch out across the wire. Without the soap the force acting across the surface of the water would pull it into a droplet.

Only a small amount of soap is needed to make bubbles in this way. Adding too much soap is less effective. Another chemical substance called glycerol makes a better bubble mixture. Food manufacturers often use glycerol. It is termed a hygroscopic liquid because it soaks up water. When glycerol is added to a bubble solution, it soaks up water molecules in the film and keeps them from evaporating too quickly. As a result, bubbles made from water and glycerol are stronger and last longer than those made from water and soap.

You can make huge bubbles like this one if you add a little glycerol or corn syrup to your bubble solution.

ACTIVITY

Blowing Bubbles

Goals

1. **Look at the way that water molecules are attracted to each other in a film of soap.**

What you will need:

- water
- tablespoon
- teaspoon
- dishwashing liquid
- bowl
- glycerol or corn syrup
- plastic plate
- drinking straws
- pipe cleaners

1 Put 10 tablespoons of water into a bowl. Then add one tablespoon of dishwashing liquid.

2 Add one teaspoon of glycerol or corn syrup to the bowl. Stir the mixture.

3 Transfer a few tablespoons of the bubble solution onto the plastic plate.

Soap

Grease forms stubborn stains on our clothes, the floor, and even our skin. Water alone is not a good cleaning agent because water molecules and grease molecules repel one another. Soaps are excellent cleaning agents. Soap is made from the fats of animals or vegetables that have been mixed with other chemicals. One end of a soap molecule is attracted to water. The other end of the same molecule is attracted to grease. When we make a soapy lather, soap and water molecules attach to the grease molecules. The grease and soap can then be washed off with more water.

Troubleshooting

What if the bubbles burst too quickly?

Increase the concentration of your bubble solution by adding more glycerol (or corn syrup) and dishwashing liquid. Bubble solution also works better if you make it the day before you do the experiment.

4 Use a straw to blow through the solution on the plate to make a bubble. Look carefully at the top of the bubble. What do you see? How big a bubble can you blow? Can you blow another bubble inside the first?

5 Bend pipe cleaners to form a square shape. Use another pipe cleaner for a handle.

6 Dip the square into the bubble solution in the bowl. What happens when you blow on the square bubble?

Monster bubbles

If you want to blow really big bubbles, make a solution using ¼ cup dishwashing liquid, ½ cup glycerol, and ⅛ cup corn syrup. Pour the solution into a large bowl or pan, and tie a loop of string to use as a frame.

FOLLOW-UP Blowing bubbles

Bend pipe cleaners into different shapes, and dip them into the bubble solution. Draw the shapes that form inside the frames in your notebook. Can you predict the way the film will look for new frames? Why does a soap film form into a bubble if it is blown into the air?

Look closely at the bubbles. Can you see any liquid moving across their surfaces? What does this tell you about why the bubbles eventually burst?

Bubble solution is sensitive to changes in the amount of water vapor in the air (humidity) and also to temperature. If the bubbles you make burst very easily, try spraying the table around your experiment with water from a plant mister. As water evaporates from the table, it increases the air humidity. This lowers the air temperature and makes your bubbles last longer.

Pepper tension

Try another surface tension experiment. Pour some milk into a saucer. Sprinkle some ground black pepper onto the surface of the milk. What happens to the pepper? How do the particles arrange themselves over the surface of the milk?

Now mix a small amount of detergent with a little water. Just add a drop of the water and detergent mixture to the center of the saucer of milk. What happens to the pepper particles? Can you explain why this happens?

◼ *Try to make bubbles of different shapes by bending the pipe cleaner in different ways. How many different ways can you make a square bubble?*

◼ *Put a piece of white paper in the bottom of the dish. You can then make measurements on the paper and use them to find out how big your bubbles are.*

ANALYSIS

Bubble science

When you blow into the bubble solution, the air you exhale forms inside a film of soapy water. The water molecules in the bubble are all attracted to one another and pull themselves into as small a space as possible. This is, in fact, the spherical shape of a bubble.

If you look closely at the top of the bubbles, you will see different colors swirling around on the surface of the soapy film. The colors are caused by light reflecting off the soap and glycerol in your bubble solution. As the force of gravity pulls these molecules down the sides of the bubble, the colors move down, too. The forces holding the bubble together weaken, and it eventually bursts. The black spots on the surface of the bubble are where the solution is thinnest and the bubble is weakest.

It is impossible to blow a square bubble, but you can make a round bubble square by forcing it to take the shape of the pipe cleaner frame. You can make other bubble shapes by bending the pipe cleaner into different shapes.

In the follow-up activity with milk and ground black pepper the pepper particles first spread out evenly across the surface of the milk. That is because the molecules across the surface of the milk are all attracted to each other by the same amount. When the detergent is added to the milk, the surface tension in the center of the milk is reduced. The surface tension around the edges of the saucer is still strong, so the water molecules are pulled to the edges. As the water molecules move, they take the pepper particles with them.

Hydrogen bonding

A water molecule is made up of one oxygen atom and two hydrogen atoms. A hydrogen atom joins to an oxygen atom by what is termed a covalent bond. In this type of bonding negatively charged electrons are shared between the atoms.

The distribution of electrons in water is unequal. Oxygen attracts electrons more strongly than hydrogen. As a result, there is a slightly stronger electrical charge at one end of the water molecule. This phenomenon is called polarity and is the reason why water attracts and dissolves so many substances.

The positive region in one water molecule also attracts negatively charged regions in other water molecules. Hydrogen bonds form where one hydrogen atom is shared by two other atoms (see the diagram at right). In water each molecule is hydrogen bonded to an average of 3.4 other water molecules. This has a strong effect on the physical properties of water, as shown by the activity you have just performed.

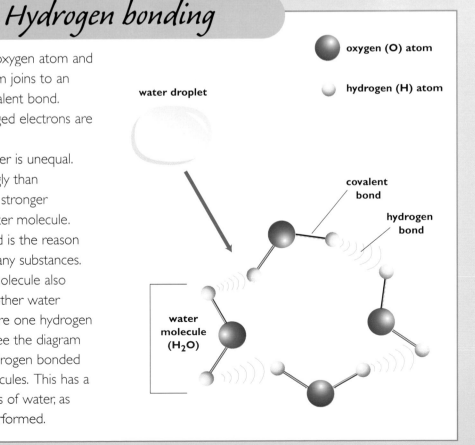

oxygen (O) atom

hydrogen (H) atom

water droplet

covalent bond

hydrogen bond

water molecule (H_2O)

ACTIVITY 10
ELECTROLYSIS

Electricity can flow through liquids that have charged particles dissolved in them. The particles can be extracted from the liquid by electrolysis. Electrolysis is used to make many things from toasters to rocket fuel.

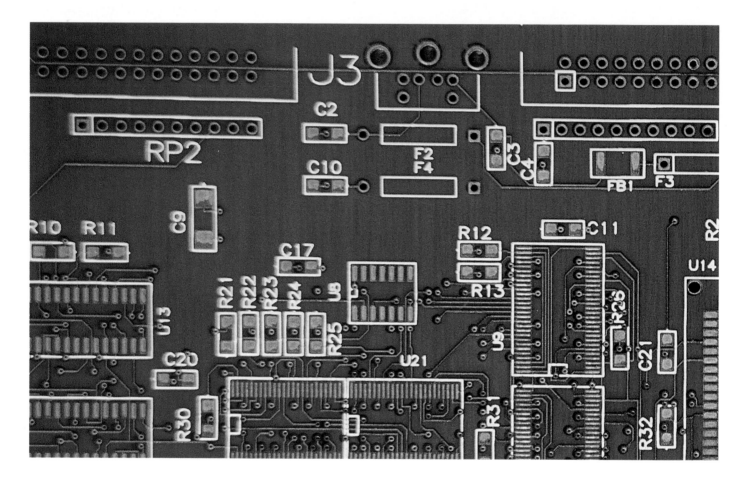

Inside every atom are a number of smaller particles called electrons, protons, and neutrons. The protons and neutrons form the nucleus at the center of the atom, while the electrons move around the nucleus. Each element (substance that cannot be broken down into other things) has a set number of particles. All atoms of the same element normally have the same number of protons and electrons. However, when an atom gains or loses electrons, it becomes an ion. Ions have either a positive or a negative charge. If the ion is missing an electron, it has a positive charge; and if it has gained an electron, it

● *Circuit boards, like the one above, are made by electroplating metal onto plastic. This creates thin metal lines that conduct currents of electricity.*

has a negative charge. Positive and negative ions are attracted to each other. When they are dissolved in a liquid, the ions can conduct an electric current, which has many uses.

Many chemicals, such as salt, are made of ions. Salt is made of sodium and chlorine ions. When salt is put into water, the ions separate from each other and dissolve. By passing a current through the salty water, the two different ions can be collected, making pure sodium metal and chlorine gas. This process is called electrolysis, and it is used to purify metals and to produce oxygen from water. Objects can be coated with a thin layer of metal using a process called electroplating, which is a type of electrolysis.

The rods that carry electricity into the liquid during electrolysis are called electrodes. The positive electrode is called the anode, and the negative one is called the cathode. The liquid holding the ions is called the electrolyte. When electricity flows through the electrolyte, ions with a positive charge are attracted to the cathode, and those with a negative charge are attracted to the anode.

SHINE ON

Electrolysis is sometimes used to cover objects with a fine layer of metal. For example, a piece of jewelry made from an inexpensive material can be given a covering of gold or silver by connecting it to an electrode. During electrolysis the precious metal ions dissolved in the electrolyte will then be attracted to the jewelry and cover its surface. This technique is called electroplating.

🔲 *This Oscar statue is being dried with compressed air after being plated with gold. The statues are plated using a type of electrolysis.*

Splitting water

Electrolysis can be used to split water, which is a compound of oxygen and hydrogen, into oxygen gas and hydrogen gas. You could do this yourself by using as electrodes two pencils that have been sharpened at both ends. Place them in a glass of salt water. Use cardboard with holes punched in it to hold the pencils upright. The pencils should not touch.

Use two electrical wires with alligator clips on each end to connect the pencils to a 9-volt battery. The alligator clips must be attached to the leads not the wooden part of the pencils.

Soon you should see bubbles around the underwater pencil leads. Hydrogen bubbles will form at the negative electrode, and oxygen gas will form at the positive electrode. There will be more hydrogen than oxygen.

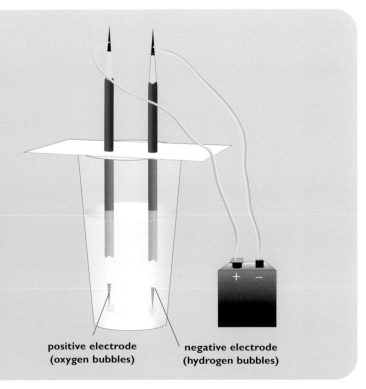

positive electrode
(oxygen bubbles)

negative electrode
(hydrogen bubbles)

Electroplating Metals

Goals

1. **Use electrolysis to plate zinc onto copper.**

What you will need:

- *2 pennies*
- *piece of sandpaper*
- *pint of vinegar*
- *glass beaker*
- *toothbrush*
- *toothpaste*
- *scales*
- *Epsom salts*
- *sugar*
- *2 electrical wires (with alligator clips)*
- *9-volt battery*

1 Using sandpaper, sand down one of the pennies until some of the copper surface is removed and the zinc (dull gray color) is exposed. It is easiest to sand the sides.

2 Clean the second penny with a toothbrush and toothpaste until it is very shiny. Rinse the penny well in water after cleaning, and be careful not to get fingerprints or other dirt on the penny.

3 Pour the vinegar into the beaker. Put the sanded-down penny into the vinegar, and let it sit for at least an hour. Some of the zinc metal will dissolve as ions in the vinegar, and you should see tiny bubbles of gas coming off the penny.

58

4 Remove the penny from the vinegar. Add 1.5 ounces (50g) of Epsom salts and 2 ounces (60g) of sugar to the vinegar, and stir until it is all dissolved.

5 Clip one electrical wire to the cleaned penny and the second wire to the sanded penny.

6 Place both pennies in the vinegar. Make sure the pennies are not touching each other.

Water on the Moon

Scientists are trying hard to find evidence of ice under the surface of the Moon, which could make building a base there much easier. The ice could be broken down, using electrolysis, into oxygen and hydrogen. People need oxygen to breathe, and hydrogen is a good fuel for making electricity. The two gases are also used as rocket fuel. Maybe one day a Moon base will be the first stop on expeditions to deep space.

7 Connect the wire clipped to the clean penny to the negative terminal on the battery. Attach the other wire to the positive terminal. After 10 minutes disconnect the battery, and carefully remove the pennies. The cleaned penny should have a bright silvery coating on it.

FOLLOW-UP Electroplating metals

There are many ways to electroplate metals onto different materials. Many of these methods, particularly the ones involving silver and gold, use dangerous and corrosive chemicals. However, you can easily plate copper onto other metals using a solution of copper sulfate. Copper sulfate can be purchased from a teaching supply store or can sometimes be found in aquarium supply stores—it is used to kill algae in ornamental ponds. Copper sulfate is poisonous; always have an adult present, and do not get the powder or liquid near your mouth or nose.

What you will need:
distilled water
copper sulfate crystals
beaker or jar
measuring spoon
two electrical wires
9-volt battery
object to plate, such as a key
copper penny

1 Make up a solution of copper sulfate by mixing 2 teaspoons of copper sulfate powder with 1 cup of distilled water. Pour the blue liquid into a beaker or jar.

2 Attach one end of an electrical wire to the end of the object you want to plate. Attach the end of the second wire to the copper penny. Put both the objects into the beaker.

3 Connect the wire coming from the object you want to plate to the negative terminal of the battery. Connect the lead coming from the copper penny to the positive terminal.

4 After about 10 minutes the object (the letter "B" here)

should be completely covered in copper. Disconnect the battery, and remove the plated object and the penny.

before   after

ANALYSIS

Electrolysis

In this activity you used electricity to attach one metal to another. All modern pennies are made from a thin layer of copper plated onto a thicker layer of zinc. (Pennies were once solid copper, but that was found to be too expensive.) By sanding the penny, you should have been able to remove enough copper to expose the zinc underneath. When you placed the sanded penny in vinegar, the zinc reacted with the vinegar, and a solution (liquid with dissolved ions) of zinc ions was formed.

By adding Epsom salts to the vinegar, you increased its ability to conduct electricity. That is because Epsom salt is also an ion, so it can carry an electric current. Table salt (sodium chloride) would have also worked, but it gives off chlorine gas, which can be very dangerous if it is breathed in. Therefore, the electrolyte was made up of positively charged zinc ions and negatively charged Epsom salt ions.

The sugar is added to the electrolyte as a brightener, to make the final zinc coating look shinier. You cleaned the other penny to remove any oils and dirt that would have kept the zinc from sticking to the copper.

Once in the solution, the sanded penny and the cleaned penny became two electrodes. Once connected to the battery, an electrical charge flowed through them. As the current flowed, the positively charged zinc ions were attracted to the negative electrode (the cleaned penny), while the negatively charged epsom salt ions were attracted to the zinc inside the sanded penny. As more and more zinc ions were attracted to the copper, it became coated (plated) in zinc.

In the follow-up activity you used dissolved copper sulfate as the electrolyte. Once dissolved, the copper sulfate became positive copper ions and negative sulfate ions. The copper penny was the positive electrode, and the object you plated was the negative electrode. Once the current was switched on, positive copper ions flowed from the solution to the negatively charged object.

Uses of electroplating

One of the metals most commonly electroplated is chrome, which is another name for the element chromium. Decorative chrome plating is also called nickel-chrome plating because it always includes plating nickel before plating the chrome. When you look at a chrome-plated truck bumper or toaster, most of what you are seeing is actually the nickel. The chrome protects against tarnishes and scratching, and adds a reflective, decorative surface.

Chrome plating starts with the object being polished and cleaned. Then it is dipped in acid (a corrosive chemical) and plated with copper. The copper is cleaned and dipped in acid again before being plated with different types of nickel and then finally with chrome.

GLOSSARY

acid: A substance that reacts with water to form hydrogen ions. Acids are sour and corrosive (attack materials).

alkali: A substance that forms hydroxide ions (an atom of oxygen and an atom of hydrogen) in water. Also called a base.

anode: Positive electrode.

atmosphere: The layer of gas surrounding Earth.

atom: The basic unit of an element and the smallest particle that has the chemical properties of the element.

bond (chemical): The attractive force between two or more atoms.

cathode: Negative electrode.

catalyst: A chemical that starts or speeds up a chemical reaction but is not changed during the reaction.

charged particle: A particle with either a positive or negative electric charge.

chemical reaction: The process in which atoms share their electrons, thus creating bonds between them. In chemical reactions bonds in

compounds may be broken and new ones made to create new substances.

chlorophyll: A green substance in the leaves of plants that traps sunlight.

colloid: Another name for an emulsion.

compound: A substance containing atoms of more than one element.

condensation: The process by which a gas, such as water vapor, turns to liquid.

covalent bond: A bond in which two or more atoms share electrons.

decantation: Pouring off a solution from one container to another without disturbing the sediment at the bottom.

density: How tightly the matter in a substance is packed together. Density is the mass of a substance compared with its volume.

distillation: The process by which a liquid is purified by heating it so that a vapor (gas) is formed. The vapor is then cooled and condenses as a liquid.

electrode: Rods that carry electricity during the process of electrolysis.

electrolysis: The process in which an electric current is passed through a liquid to separate out certain ions.

electrolyte: The liquid that holds the ions during the process of electrolysis.

electromagnetic radiation: Energy in wave form, including light, radio waves, x-rays, infrared, ultraviolet, and other waves.

electron: A charged particle that orbits the nucleus (center) of an atom.

electroplating: A type of electrolysis during which objects are coated with a thin layer of metal.

element: A substance that cannot be broken down into simpler substances using chemicals. An element contains only one kind of atom.

emulsion: A suspension that can stay mixed without separating into layers.

evaporate: To change from a liquid into a gas, for example, by boiling water.

hydrometer: A device that measures the specific gravity of a liquid.

immiscible liquids: Those liquids that cannot be dissolved into each other but can be mixed in other ways.

ion: An atom that is part of a compound and that has either lost or gained electrons. An atom that has lost electrons is called a cation; an atom that gained electrons is an anion.

ionic bond: A bond in which atoms gain or lose one or more electrons.

mass: A measure of the amount of matter that an object contains.

matter: Any object or substance that has mass.

miscible liquids: Liquids that can be dissolved into each other.

molecule: A group of atoms that share electrons—they are bonded together.

nonpolar molecule: A molecule in which the electrons are spaced out evenly all around it.

nucleus: The center of an atom. The nucleus contains smaller particles called protons and neutrons.

oxidation: Gaining atoms of oxygen or losing electrons during a chemical reaction.

phase: Another name for a state of matter.

physics: The study of the physical properties of matter and of the physical changes that take place between matter and energy.

photosynthesis: The process by which plants use sunlight to turn carbon dioxide and water into sugars for food.

polar molecule: A molecule in which the electrons are spaced out unevenly.

pressure: The amount of force exerted by a substance, for example, air, measured at a particular place.

quantum: The smallest unit of energy. A quantum of light energy is a photon.

redox reaction: A chemical reaction with two parts— reduction and oxidation.

reduction: Losing oxygen atoms or gaining electrons during a chemical reaction.

respiration: The process by which living organisms release energy from food.

saturated solution: A solution that can hold no more of a solute at a given temperature and pressure.

solubility: A measure of the maximum amount of solute that will dissolve in a solvent at a given temperature.

solute: Dissolved substance.

solution: A liquid containing two or more substances dissolved in it.

solvent: Any substance that is able to dissolve another substance.

stationary phase (in chromatography): The material across which the substance that is to be separated moves.

suspension: A mixture of liquids in which droplets of an immiscible liquid float in another liquid. Many suspensions are temporary— the droplets separate into a distinct layer.

volume: A measure of the space that an object takes up.

weight: A measure of how strongly gravity pulls an object toward Earth. Weight and mass are not the same thing—objects have the same mass wherever they are, but they may not weigh the same. For example, a bar of steel would weigh less in space than it does on Earth.

SET INDEX